August 2019

BURNED

My Journey Through Addiction

Thank you Andi for your
friendship and for always
encouraging and supporting
me.
I am blessed to have
you in my life.
Keep loving on your grandsons
and I know you and Bob
are where you belong.

JANA ROE

XX OO

Jana

ISBN 978-1-64349-614-6 (paperback)
ISBN 978-1-64349-613-9 (digital)

Christian Faith Publishing, Inc.
832 Park Avenue
Meadville, PA 16335
www.christianfaithpublishing.com

Printed in the United States of America

DEDICATION

I AM PRIVILEGED TO DEDICATE my book to the following people:

My loving and supportive family, which includes my husband Wayne, my daughter Stacy, and my son David.

Dr. Ashish Bhatia for putting action behind his support. I am grateful for his guidance, his dedication to helping others and for his contribution to my book.

Dr. Amanda Friedrichs and Dr. Fred Kemp, thank you for saving my life and for changing my life forever.

My friends Monica and Becky, thank you for allowing me to share my story with others and for believing in me.

My friend/sister in Christ, Becky, for taking the time to read my story before anyone else did and to give me her powerful, uplifting message of faith.

My friend Cathy for giving me the power of "I can." She was the one who started me on my path of speaking. Thank you, Cathy, for empowering me.

My friend Andi who is always there to lend an ear and to make me laugh.

My friend Jessica for being brave enough to stop her addiction to tanning after hearing my story.

The teachers and students that I have been privileged to speak to, thank you for all your heartfelt letters, your support, and for giving me the chance to share my story. I am touched by your kindness, and I will continue to make a difference in the life of others.

FOREWORD

THIS IS MY MOTHER'S STORY about hardship, struggle, and overcoming the odds. It may be strange for a daughter to write the foreword to her mom's book, but we are different. We know everything about each other, down to the darkest secrets. Some may see this as a book about skin cancer, and it is, but it is also so much more than that. We all have struggles that no one sees on the outside that we are fighting within us. We just need to look and have empathy.

I was blessed to be raised by flawed people. Perfection is not attainable and should not be a goal for anyone. The flaws make you who you are. Addiction is real and palpable in my family. That can mean drugs, medication, alcohol, and tanning. I would see my dad drinking and understood he had a problem. He rectified that and stopped drinking years ago. So many memories of my mom are of her out in the sun. I would have friends over, and she would be outside in a bikini always in the sun. I always wanted to help and say, "STOP." Sometimes I did as a child, but that was not her time to face the addiction and make a change.

When I really think about how society has become all about the external and not the internal, it makes my soul hurt. All I want to say is "Love yourself." Struggle with self-esteem and self-worth is something my mom and I have spoken about in-depth. The concept of being thin, tanned, and "perfect" was appealing to my mom at a young age.

We all have choices that come before us, and how we respond shapes us. The one thing that no one really talks about is that when you know you need to make a change the path it takes you down. This book is a path. There is beauty, pain, turmoil, and all other fluctuating emotions. If you or a loved one are in the midst of addiction, there is always hope. My parents both proved that to me.

Stacy Roe

"You, O Lord keep my lamp burning; my
God turns my darkness into light."
—Psalm 18:28

"You are the light of the world. A town built on a hill cannot
be hidden. Neither do people light a lamp and put it under a bowl.
Instead they put it on its stand, and it gives light to everyone in the
house. In the same way, let your light shine before others, that they
may see your good deeds and glorify your Father in heaven."
—Matthew 5:14–16

PROLOGUE

BEING A DERMATOLOGIST AND A dermatologic surgeon, every day I have the privilege of people trusting me to help them with their skin issues. These issues most often include skin cancers, sun damage, birthmarks, burns, scars, and aging. Since skin cancers are the most common cancers in humans, it is not unusual for us to treat many skin cancers every day. The effects of skin cancer can range from annoying to disfiguring to deadly. As each person is an individual, so is each skin cancer based upon its aggressiveness, its location, and its size. Though it is easy to see what effect skin cancers and precancerous lesions have on people's skin, what isn't apparent to the casual observer is the impact of these issues on our patients' lives. To some, it is simply a nuisance, to others, their skin cancers and precancerous spots can be steeped with feelings of guilt, hopelessness, or worse.

Besides being their doctor, for most patients I also play the role of a guide. Being a guide is an important and integral role of caring for a person diagnosed with a skin cancer. How to guide someone through this is not taught in medical school, and there is no one right way to do it. Each person with skin cancer has a different journey, a different path, and a different experience through their treatment and recovery. Because of this, guiding each person through his or her experiences must be done on an individual basis. One of the better possible outcomes of guiding someone is when the patient is cured of the immediate disease *and* the patient is able to take the experience and use it to break the habits and behaviors which contributed to the disease. In the case of skin cancer, this includes practicing sun protection (sun protective clothing, sunscreen and sun glasses), sun avoidance, and getting regular skin checks. However, once in a rare while, an exceptional thing happens: a patient takes his or her experiences, and uses them to educate and help others. For some, this even becomes their calling, their *raison d'être*.

This book is not about skin cancer. It is not about addiction. What it is about is one person's journey through a life which was affected by both skin cancer and addiction. More importantly, it is about hope, transformation and finding one's path. I hope the journey detailed in this book will help others find their own path and avoid some of life's pitfalls.

You would expect a physician to tell you to take care of yourself, because without your health, it becomes more difficult to do the things you love and to help others. I will leave you with a notion that has been very instrumental in my life. These words were shared by the President of Illinois Wesleyan University, Dr. Minor Myers, Jr., at our graduation. "Go into the world and do WELL, but more importantly, go into the world and do GOOD." I'd like to add to this: Don't forget to wear your sunscreen, sun protective hats & clothing, and sunglasses too!

Ashish C. Bhatia, MD, FAAD
Associate Professor of Clinical Dermatology
Northwestern University, Feinberg School of Medicine, Chicago, IL

Co-Director of Dermatologic, Laser & Cosmetic Surgery
& Director of Clinical Research, Oak Dermatology, Schaumburg, IL

CHAPTER 1

I AM BROKEN. BUT DON'T misconstrue that to mean that I am weak because I am strong. I was a victim as a child of my circumstances, but I am not a victim; I am a victor. This is not a self-help book, but instead, this is my journey. I do not have all the answers to how a person can overcome any addiction; this is my story about how I found light in the darkness of my own addiction. Each person with an addiction is uniquely different; however, we are locked together because of the power we give the monster that lives inside of us. I know for me I gave my addiction so much power that I felt weak and defeated against it. My addiction had me trapped; it was easier to give in than to fight it. I gave in at an early age that this was my life and I had no control over anything, but I couldn't have been farther from the truth. I had the ability all along to change my course, but that only came after I saw the light, the true light, the only light that shines on this world, my Lord and savior Jesus Christ. Because I was given the "light," I am able to pass it on to others and hopefully they see the true "light" that lives within me.

CHAPTER 2

MY ADDICTION BEGAN WHEN I was ten years old, and yes, I had a traumatic event happen at that age, but that is not what I focus on in my journey. My addiction was to tanning, and at that young age, I saw that people see what is on the outside long before they see what beauty is on the inside. I remember taking out of our crowded, small garage a single woven lawn chair, the kind that is a tri-fold, and putting it on the patio in our backyard. It was a small, square concrete patio that at one corner held a basketball hoop, which I spent many hours using, but not when I wanted to feel "pretty" and "accepted" by others. I was starved for attention, and this was the one thing, the only thing that I had control over as a young child. Everything else in my world was dictated by an adult, and this was my way to escape to feel powerful even though it gave me a false sense of security. I remember putting on my bikini, which I loved because I could wear it many different ways (that's the way they used to make them) and I was able to get much of my body to a different color, a color that I thought made me look beautiful. I took with me a small bottle of baby oil, which I drenched my skin in to make the sun beat down even more intense on my "tough skin" or so I thought. It became very obvious to me that I could spend hours tossing and turning to cover every inch of myself in a deep, brilliant red color, which went from the top of my head to the ends of my toes. I didn't tan as a child; I burned, but it made me feel good to have the pain of doing something that I felt so proud of, and no one could control that—only I could. When I was younger, no one saw a dermatologist for anything. If you had acne, put some Clearasil on it and that was the solution to your problem. I remember seeing posters in the locker room at school on smoking, but I never saw a poster on the dangers of tanning. It was something that no one talked or warned you about. In middle school, I went with a friend of mine to their family's beach house. I liked an older boy and the only way to get him to notice me "in my eyes" was to be pretty and that meant burning my skin to a crisp to the point of basking in the sun for eight hours. By the time I was done, I could not even sit down because I was raw, and it still didn't get him to pay attention to me. I did this on several occasions and not just for a boy but for me and my self-image issues.

CHAPTER 3

I AM FIFTY-SIX YEARS OLD, and I still have self-image issues with the way I look. When I was younger, I would lay out, in fact I did it as often as I could. If my trusty chair was being occupied by my mom, I would lay on the picnic table—anything to make me look better, different than me. I am trying hard to remember what my skin originally looked like, but to no avail. I loved being outside and I never ever wore sunscreen, sat in the shade, or wore clothes to protect my skin (i.e., a hat, long sleeves). The sun was my friend, and it helped me to feel better about who I was, even if it was only temporary, and it was just that. How I wish I could go back in time to heal the little girl that was once me. I would hold her tight and tell her, "You are beautiful just the way you are," but that cannot happen and I am left with the consequences of my actions that started at the age of ten. Even though as a child, I did not know that I was addicted to tanning, by the time I was in my twenties, I had come to the realization that this was how I was going to die. At the time, it gave me great comfort that I didn't have to worry about "how," I just didn't know "when." People that knew me as I was growing up, and even into my twenties, thirties, and forties, did not realize that by giving me "compliments" about how tan I was that they were actually "feeding" my addiction. Please be very clear on this; it is not their fault. The only person I blame for my actions is myself, no one else. I battled anorexia in my twenties but that was short-lived. I did like the control, though, and like my tanning addiction, every time I looked in the mirror, I never saw myself as "pretty," "skinny enough," or "tan enough." I could never fill the hole that was missing in me. I tried many ways to fill the emptiness and loneliness of not having many friends and not being shown affection or made to feel pretty by my parents, but I failed each and every time. I was self-destructive in the way I treated my skin. I had a summer job detassling corn when I was in tenth and eleventh grade. The picture of me my junior year of high school was the best one I had ever taken. In fact boys started to notice me and peers started to pay attention to me and give me positive feedback on the way I looked. I was convinced that the only way for me to "have friends" or "have boyfriends" was to be tan all the time. Even my addiction was telling me, "You're only pretty if you are tan" and "People only like you when you are tan." The voice in my head became stronger and stronger each day.

CHAPTER 4

MY FIRST CHOICE WAS ALWAYS to lay outside to get a tan. I'm not sure at what age I started using indoor tanning beds, but I was amazed that I could get "sunburned" within twenty minutes instead of laying out for hours, literally. I didn't like wasting my time once I got there. I wanted to know two things. First, what room number will I be in (because I did have my favorites) and how many minutes do I have left. Anything else was aggravating and kept me from having my relaxation time.

I was twenty years old when I married my husband. I know, that's so young, right? But he saved me and he loved me even though I could not understand why. I became pregnant when I was halfway between the age of twenty-one and twenty-two years old. I had a serious dilemma, and even though I was thrilled to have a baby, I had an addiction, and like any addict, I needed to get my "fix." I still laid out when I was pregnant with my daughter, but I covered my stomach with my swimsuit. It wasn't what I wanted to do, but I knew no one wanted to see my large, stretched-out belly. I remember after my daughter was born taking her to tanning salons. I left her with the people who worked there while I satisfied my need for the sun, even if it was fake. I recall the way I felt when I went inside the room; they always had the palm tree decorations to simulate a beach setting and the way I felt when I laid inside them was like a little kid getting a piece of candy—complete satisfaction. The one and only good thing that I did when I indoor tanned was I always wore the goggles to protect my eyes. I remember stripping down to my bikini swimsuit, and being cold when I first lay on the glass bottom. Once I was ready, I pushed a button and I was transformed to a beach, the wind (actually a fan) blowing at the top of my head and the bottoms of my feet. Most of all, I remember the warmth that spread over me and I could imagine myself being in a tropical location until the buzzer rang and my time was over. I never felt bad at the time for taking my daughter with me, and even though I'm sure the people who ran the salon didn't like that I brought her, they knew they had a good customer that was always aching to come back. I needed to lay out, and so when my daughter took a nap, I would be outside our mobile home, soaking up the rays. Even if she didn't sleep, I needed to do this; it wasn't a "want" in my eyes, it was a "need." If I was to be a good mother, I had to feel good about myself and there was only one way to get that done—to be tan. No rain, no cloudy weather, or even the winter could stop me now; I had year-round exposure. I had no idea that just over twenty years later, I would live to regret the choices I made.

Chapter 5

My son was born five and a half years after my daughter. As with my daughter, I had to lay out even if it meant I had to cover up my stomach. During both pregnancies, I did not indoor tan. It was harder for me to lay out when I had both children, but I managed as well as I could. I did the same thing with my son that I did with my daughter; as soon as he went down for a nap, and it was sixty degrees or warmer, I would be outside. As I got older, I stopped using the baby oil, and I either used water or I started buying tanning lotions to enhance my "glow." Any time we had plans to do anything such as go to a park, visit relatives, etc., I would have to be able to tan before we left or my entire day was ruined. If it became cloudy outside, my demeanor would change and I would be instantly crabby and irritable. I built my life around my addiction—that came first, above everyone and everything. Believe me when I say I'm embarrassed for the way I was, but this was my life. I am not proud of what I did, but I have nothing to hide. I practically lived in my bathing suit in the summer time. We went on many vacations when my kids were young, especially to—you guessed it—a beach. I have pictures of me with my kids and I'm in between them with my bikini on and every inch of me tan. I hardly have any pictures of me without a tan; that's the only way I wanted to see myself. Anything else was unacceptable to me. I would put sunscreen on my kids, but I never put any on me. I didn't want to wear it because I was afraid it would inhibit my tan, and it would keep the beautiful sun's rays from making me golden brown. I didn't want anything to keep me from being as tan as I possibly could be. As I stated earlier, I regarded my skin as being "tough." When we went to the beach, I didn't play with my children; that was always my husband's job. My one and only concern was soaking up the rays. My kids would run around and play, and I would be paying close attention to how long I had tanned on one side and when I would have to turn over. I didn't lay out for one, two, or even three hours it was an all-day marathon. There were a few times that my husband got sun poisoning, and I would laugh and tell him how much tougher my skin was than his. It never bothered me because I didn't let anyone else's circumstances affect what I needed to do. My first priority was to be tan, plain and simple.

CHAPTER 6

As MY CHILDREN GREW OLDER, my addiction became more and more defined. If they wanted friends to come over, I told them to stay inside because I was tanning in the backyard. I didn't stop tanning, and I know how overcome with embarrassment they felt, but at the time, I didn't care. Nothing could stop me and nothing could get in my way. I started to add music outside to help with the boredom, and I even bought a baby pool, not for my kids but for me. I would get so hot and that would help cool me down so that I could stay out even longer. We put up a six-foot high wooden fence in our yard right after our son was born. It was for our pets, but it was mainly for me. I wanted and required privacy, and I wanted to walk around in my bikini all the time, in the spring and summer. I even washed my car with my bikini top on and a pair of shorts. Being out in the sun and getting browner was the biggest goal I had. We had gone on a trip to sunny Arizona in the middle of summer, a tanning addict's biggest thrill. My husband had a spot on his back, and I noticed it was starting to change. When we came home, I told him he should probably have a doctor take a look at it. They did a biopsy of the area, and it came back pre-malignant melanoma. He had a large area cut out of his back, and I got all over him to start wearing sunscreen and to protect himself, but I never said those words to me. I never saw how it could affect me and it gave me a reason to once again tell him that my skin was better and tougher than his. Never did I have empathy; he just didn't have strong enough skin. My skin was tough, I thought; I made it that way.

CHAPTER 7

I TALKED EARLIER ABOUT MY self-image and that I still have issues with my looks today. I don't think I explained to you how deep it goes. I look in my mirror in the morning to get ready for the day, but in any bathroom that I use throughout the day other than my own, I don't look at myself. I don't like what I see and to make me feel better I just don't look straight on. It is my issue and something that I will either resolve someday or it will be the way things are. Either way, it doesn't upset me; it is just how I cope. Even though my addiction is gone, some of the effects linger on and this is one of them. I also have a hard time accepting a compliment, especially on the way I look. I don't see what everyone else does. I only see my mistakes and imperfections and I have my addiction to blame for that. Something that goes along with self-image is self-worth. Mine is damaged and the self-talk I hear in my head has always been "You're not good enough, pretty enough, smart enough," etc., and the negativity distorts everything. Like my addiction, the self-talk always kept me searching for a way to make "me" feel better. But like my tan would fade away, so would the temporary good thoughts that I had when I looked in the mirror as I noticed my skin fading back to reality. Tanning did not come easy for me. Because my skin is naturally fair, I had to work harder than most people on getting and maintaining that look. I remember many times my children coming into the bathroom and telling me that I looked like an "Indian" and I was so happy when they said that. I would always say, "Thank you,

I wish I was." But when I looked in the mirror, I didn't see what they saw; I only saw disappointment again and again. I could never obtain what I really wanted and that was to be someone different, anyone but me. I ran from myself and that's why my addiction fooled me. I considered it to be a very controlling friend running my life from the inside of my head. The trickery would last for decades and the price was too high. I did not find that out until it was almost too late.

CHAPTER 8

I WAS A GOOD MOM, but I had an addiction. Some people have asked me if what I had was really an addiction and when I look up the definition here is what I found in dictionary.com: "*the state of being enslaved to a habit or practice or to something that is psychologically or physically habit-forming.*" Yes, I can honestly say I had an addiction, but I don't understand how someone who didn't live my life had the gall to ask me that question. I laid out in my back yard with my six-foot high wooden fence protecting me, but as I got older and especially as my children grew, my addiction grew also. I no longer had the small children to take care of, and as my kids gained their independence, my dependence to tanning was putting its grip on me. I also started to ask my husband and daughter to spend time with me, enjoying what I love to do most. I would ask my husband to indoor and outdoor tan with me and he would sometimes humor me by laying outside with me, but he never went to a salon. My daughter was my "main focus." I wanted her to be just like me and I started becoming a bully towards her. I would say "I'm bored, come lay out with me" or "Are you chicken, are you afraid of the sun, don't you want to be pretty like me?" I tried everything I could think of to either guilt her or bully her to step with me down the path of self-destruction. I am so proud of my daughter for never giving in to my persuasion. She would come back with comments such as "That's your addiction, not mine" or "You're going to die from skin cancer, not me." My comeback line to that was always the same "As long as

21

I die tan." I said that to both my son and my daughter more times than I can remember. Those were the words I was willing to stand on. When I think of it now, it makes me feel sad that I couldn't see their pain. I was so proud of myself for putting them "in their place" because in my mind I was sticking up for two people, myself, and my addiction.

CHAPTER 9

LET ME GO THROUGH SOME of my tanning rituals with you. As soon as I woke up in the morning, I would look outside (I mean through my open door) to see if it was sunny and look for any clouds that could potentially put me in a "bad mood." If it was sunny and at least sixty degrees I would run upstairs, brush my teeth, and pull my hair up so it would be completely off my skin. I would then go outside in my garage, get my one and only favorite laying out chair, and turn on the radio so that I could hear the music playing from inside the garage. I would set down my chair and open it up. Then I went inside to fill up the watering can with cold water and get my tanning oil and proceed to slather it on my skin. The closer I came to actually "laying out," the happier and childlike I found myself getting. I had a small watch that I could view without straining myself and I put a large beach towel on my chair covering up the slits in-between the openings. I had to carefully plan my time. I always started by laying on my back first. I would move my arms the opposite way after fifteen minutes of "complete" sun on them. If it became cloudy, I would have to adjust for that factor. I would also move my legs from straight down to the outside and then to the inside for fifteen minutes each. My face received the same treatment. I usually gave my front face thirty minutes then I would turn to each side for fifteen minutes. I kept repeating this ritual until I felt done on the front and only then would I lay on my stomach. I never did any routine for my back side, but I did stay in that direction for at least forty-five to sixty minutes. I would completely relax unless the pesky clouds got in the way. I did not wear sunscreen or sunglasses ever. I didn't want any marks left on my face so I laid out protection-free. I have to be honest; after writing down my steps, I'm exhausted. I don't know how I did this all the time. When I was finished and I felt satisfied with my success, I would come in and take a shower. The feelings that came over me were "accomplishment" and "fulfillment." I was always proud of myself for sticking to the regime I created for this ritual, and it was probably the only time I felt content. If someone came over when I was still outside, I would become irritated. I'm sure it was easy to tell from the expression on my face that I was not happy to see them, or in my opinion bothered by them. When I went to bed at night, I always checked the weather for the next day. Even though I worked at a job, as soon as I got home, I would try to shorten my "desired time" to give every part of my body "full sun" opportunity. This scheduling was a huge part of my addiction. Everything had to be just right in order for me to be happy. Any glitch would throw me off, and if the clouds became too thick, I would jump in my car and finish my session indoors without any interruptions.

CHAPTER 10

EVEN THOUGH IT HAS BEEN many years since I went to a tanning salon, there are things I still remember. Going there made me feel so good and I did not want to be bothered with anyone; just give me the room number and tell me how many minutes I could tan. Those were my inner thoughts. Once a year, they had me sign a waiver that said, "Tanning causes skin cancer, and if I got it, I wouldn't sue them." I signed that piece of paper without batting an eye. That wasn't going to happen to me, that happens to other people is what kept going through my head. My one and only focus was to get in the room and feel better about the way I looked. I was a very selfish person, not that I still don't have those moments now, but I was a different person. I didn't care about what others wanted, only myself. Ugly insecurity started to show itself to me. I started comparing myself to others (especially women) if I saw them tan. I began to personally challenge myself to be better than them at any cost. If it meant I would have to lay out longer or more often, I had to "win" the contest that was only in my head. No one else knew about it because I didn't say anything out loud. It was another way my addiction cost me, and because of my low self-esteem, I couldn't challenge it. I needed to be the center of attention. I remember when my daughter was getting married in June of 2010. I had my hair colored and I had been working on my tan all week long for the big event. At her bachelorette party, I noticed one of her friends who was standing up for her was tanner than me. She became my competition and I told my daughter that I would be indoor tanning the next day because I wasn't "tan enough." She told me, "Please stop, Mom, you're so dark, please don't." I didn't want her friend to be the focus of attention on the day of the wedding and I had to be prettier and tanner than everyone else. My dress was a soft yellow, but when I look back at pictures of me that day, there is nothing soft about what was happening to my skin. My years of worshipping the sun were numbered, and I didn't know it.

CHAPTER 11

AT MY DAUGHTER'S WEDDING IN June of 2010, I had a great time dancing and feeling like I was on top of the world. In October of 2010, I was taking a shower and I felt a spot on my upper back. I couldn't see it, but I had my husband look at it. He said it looked like a wart, but I waited to see if "it" would go away. The spot was still there a few weeks later, and I decided to have my general doctor take a look at it. I didn't want to be bothered so I told him to look at my spot, give me some cream, and I'll be on my way. I wasn't worried; I thought it was probably something stupid and I wasn't sure if I should even be there. His face told me he thought differently than I did. He strongly suggested that I go upstairs immediately and have a surgeon remove it. I didn't see the concern and I just wanted to leave, but because I respect his opinion, I reluctantly did as he requested. I never had something like this done before, but again I felt no need to be nervous and I checked in at the front desk. They led me back to a room and explained the procedure to me. I would be awake and they numbed the area by giving me injections around the "spot" they were going to cut. The surgeon came in and put me completely at ease by talking about my kids, and before I knew it, the whole thing was over and they told me how to care for my wound and clean my stitches. The last thing they told me was that they would be sending this away to a lab and that they would call me in five to seven days with the results. I left, thanked the doctor for making this procedure uneventful, and I walked away, not thinking about how this could affect anything in my life. I received a phone call a few days later.

CHAPTER 12

I WAS AT MY JOB and I was just getting ready to leave for the day when I received a phone call on my cell phone. I picked it up and said, "Hello" and the voice on the other side of the phone told me they were calling from the doctor's office and they had the results from the surgery. I said "Okay, what is it?"

She said, "It was basal cell carcinoma."

I told her, "I have no idea what you just said."

She said, "It's skin cancer."

Now wait a minute, this wasn't supposed to happen to me; this happens to other people! I hung up the phone and began weeping at my desk. I started to feel very sad and confused about what she said to me. But you have to remember that I had an addiction and the "little voice in my head" began talking to me.

My addiction said, "Hey, call her back. *Do* you have skin cancer, or *did* you have skin cancer?" The voice was persistent so I called the nurse right back.

I said, "I have a question: do I have skin cancer, or did I have skin cancer? I need to know." The nurse said, "You are going to be fine, the doctor got it all, and there is nothing else you need to do."

Boom! That was all I needed to hear; that's all "my addiction" needed to hear. I wasn't going to do anything different; after all, I don't have skin cancer anymore. It's gone. My short-term worry and fear completely disappeared. As my scar began to heal and I was tanning indoors, I made sure I protected that scar by having my

28

husband put a bandage on it. I wanted to make sure I kept that spot safe. The scare was over and I was back in business. My addiction won and made me see that I didn't need to worry about anything. I just needed to keep tanning because I wasn't hurting anyone. I didn't see this as a warning sign; I just saw how strong I was when I relied on my addiction to lead me.

CHAPTER 13

WE TOOK OUR KIDS TO either Florida or Arizona for vacations. Arizona was my favorite place because of the hot, sunny weather and also because we had friends who lived there. I loved visiting them, mainly because they had an outdoor pool and they didn't mind if I needed to "relax" and "sun myself" outside. Seeing them was great but because of my addiction and my need to please "myself," I looked forward to those trips the most. We went to Mexico twice, and during the first trip, I had my husband lay out with me on the white, sandy beach for close to eight hours. There were little palm tree umbrellas on the beach for people who wanted shade, but in my eyes that was for wimps and I never used them. Once again, he got sun poisoning, but that didn't stop me from "toughening" up my skin for days on end. The luxurious accommodations came in last place against the sand, water, and endless sun of this tropical destination. When we got back from vacation, I had many people tell me how relaxed and young I looked, and I knew it was because they saw my deep, gorgeous, tanned skin. It gave me a high and put me up on a pedestal (of my own creation), and it wasn't until the natural fading started creeping up on me that I would again follow my strict tanning regimen. On those trips, anytime I had to put "real clothes" on I would feel angry and cheated out of my "sun time." I was only happy hanging out on the beach or by the pool in my swimsuit. Those were the only "clothes" I wanted to wear. Anything else kept me from getting a tan all over and it made me upset. Even once the sun began to set a feeling of sadness would come over me and the only thing on my mind was waking up in the morning and heading once more to the hot, Mexican sand. I was in my early forties and I felt great, looked young and I didn't see anything changing. The skin cancer "scare" was a distant memory, and I felt alive and healthy even though my skin was "extremely sick."

CHAPTER 14

IN JULY OF 2011, MY husband and I were on a vacation by ourselves in sunny Arizona. We had a fairly nice hotel in Tucson and while my husband was staying inside our hotel room to avoid the mid-day heat, I was in and out of the swimming pool enjoying my time greatly. I didn't need anyone to be with me to have fun, but it did make me happier when others would come and join me. About five years prior, my husband had seen a small patch of dry skin on my upper thigh and commented to me about it on several occasions. He wanted me to see a doctor because no matter what kind of lotion I applied to the area, it continued to look the same. At this time and throughout our marriage, he had his own addiction to smoking. Whenever he mentioned this "spot" to me, I would say to him, "You have your own addiction, you leave me alone and I'll leave you alone." In fact, I used to joke with him and say, "We're probably going to die right down the hall from each other. You're going to die from lung cancer and I'm going to die from skin cancer." I would laugh and get my point across for him to keep his comments to himself, and it worked. He let me continue my sick addiction and I let him do the same. It worked for us because we didn't feel like we were accountable to anyone for our choices. I did worry about him smoking, but because I was so entrenched in my own addiction I was afraid that if we talked about it we might both lose what we enjoyed so much and that was too big of a risk for me to take. My kids I'm sure hated that we both had "bad, unhealthy habits" but we were both oblivious to any harm that could come to us or that our choices affected anyone. That was all about to change.

CHAPTER 15

I CAME INSIDE THE HOTEL room in Tucson and took a shower. When I came out of the shower, the "spot" that my husband was worried about had opened up and was bleeding. I immediately knew what this meant—"I had skin cancer." I walked into the bedroom where he was watching a movie and told him what I knew, what I really had always known. I cried silently and even though his arms around my body comforted me, I was not prepared for the "new normal" I was about to embark on. I knew that once we got back home, I would have to take care of this "new problem." I made an appointment with a surgeon, and he was going to take care of that area, and I also found another "spot" behind my right knee. Both of the spots were basal cell carcinoma. I was starting to see a pattern and I was becoming more aware of my skin. I noticed that my arms and hands were always "red," but when I felt uneasy about it, my addiction would tell me, "You're just doing such a great job of tanning and that I didn't have anything to be worried about." I started looking at other people and their skin did not look like mine and it made me curious enough to make an appointment with the first surgeon I had gone to. When she came into the room, I said, "I think there is something wrong with my arms and hands, they're red all the time."

She impulsively became upset with me and asked me, "Why are you making appointments to see me, what do you want me to tell you, that it's normal? It's not normal, stop making appointments to see me and set up a time to speak to a dermatologist." I was overcome with confusion. I thought she cared about me and she should know I don't want to see a "skin doctor." They would try to scare me and take away my fun. I left her office feeling let down and without any answers to my question. I thought to myself, "Isn't it her job to help me?" I was left with only one choice, the one thing that I really did not want to do, see a dermatologist. But I didn't go alone to see her, my addiction was always with me.

CHAPTER 16

I MADE THE APPOINTMENT WITH a dermatologist, but before I went, I made a pact or an agreement with my addiction. I decided that no matter what she said, I was never going to stop, there was nothing she could say to me to scare me into stopping. I also knew that the only thing I was going to have her look at were my arms and hands, nothing else. I got to her office, checked in, and then sat in the room waiting for her to come in and "evaluate" me. I felt strong because of the pact I made and I was ready for anything she was going to throw at me.

My attitude was "give it your best shot." In fact I was even a little smug and cocky as soon as I saw her peer in through the door. She came in and I made sure she knew the limits I was setting on her. I told her, "I'm only here for my arms and hands, nothing else." She walked over to me and I stood up. I let her look at me and then she went and sat down across the room. She took a moment, and I was starting to get irritated that she was wasting my precious time. Maybe there was nothing wrong, just like my addiction had been telling me. She finally spoke and she said, "I know exactly what I can do for you."

I said, "What?"

She said, "I'm going to take all the skin off from your hands and arms and replace it with new skin."

I looked shocked and I replied, "Wow, you can really do that?"

36

She firmly told me, "No, I can't do that. Don't you understand what you have done to yourself?" She also added, "I don't know if I can help you, I don't know what I can do for you, and yours is the worst case I have ever seen."

I was blown completely off my stance and then she asked me the question that still haunts me to this day. "Do you want to die from this, from skin cancer?"

I was bewildered and thought, "What's happening to me?"

I thought I was prepared for what she might throw at me, but I wasn't. I was lied to by my addiction that up until now always had a comeback line ready for me, but not this time. She stood there waiting for me to respond, and I answered her, "No, I don't want to die from this." For the first time, my addiction didn't answer, I did. My treatments started that day.

CHAPTER 17

SHE THREW A LOT AT me that day, and I was not ready to begin what has been a long, painful, and scary journey. She explained to me that my skin is badly damaged and that I had to start using a cream everywhere because I have a condition called "actinic keratosis" or pre-skin cancer all over my body. My worst areas are my hands, arms, and face. She gave me a prescription for the cream and told me I had to have a treatment on my face soon. That treatment she said is called "Photo Dynamic Therapy" or PDT for short. She was very concerned because of all the pre-cancerous spots she saw on my skin, especially on my face. I didn't know anything she was talking about, but I knew one thing; she was really scaring me. I felt alone and dazed. I had come there alone and the only thing I wanted to do was to go in my car and bawl my eyes out. I had gone from I look "great" and "young" to talk about dying. What have I done to myself? I didn't sign up for this; I was just having fun, not hurting anyone, right? I made the appointment for my face over my winter break in December 2011. I had no idea what I was in for, and exactly what starting my treatments would mean for me. I knew one thing for sure: I was an addict and more than anything right now I wish I could tan and get away from this cruel reality shock.

CHAPTER 18

I WAS TO SEE HER once a month—that was a lot. I have never seen a doctor that much in my entire life, and now I am supposed to come in and let her check me over every thirty days?? What is that about? I picked up the cream that I was to use. I don't remember the insurance portion of the cost, but I just know what I paid which was $20. I called my husband and told him the unimaginable news, while I sobbed in my car driving home. How was I going to be okay with this? How am I going to cope? Embarrassment and humiliation were with me on the drive. I had to pay someone to tell me this; should I believe her or not? Many different emotions flooded over my judgment. One part of me was feeling very sorry for myself and I didn't know why this has happened to me (as if I didn't do anything wrong) and another side of me was fighting what she said.

I remember telling friends that "She can't tell me what to do. I'll do whatever I want. I like tanning, who is she to tell me what to do?" One thing was true; I was sitting in a big, dark, empty hole and I didn't see any way out of this. I knew I had an addiction, I even told a doctor this fact about ten years prior. My son had severe acne and I found a dermatologist in another town to take him to see. It took us a year to see him after making the initial phone call. He was a sweet, older man who truly cared about my son and his patients. He took his time with us and was very helpful in finding a way to combat his acne. However, on one occasion, the doctor made a huge mistake and one I never forgot about. I was in the hallway ready to go into the room with my son and he stopped me. He pulled me to the side and told me that he was concerned about me. He could tell that I was fair-skinned, but I was so tan.

I flipped out on him, and I yelled at him and told him, "I know I have an addiction and I'm okay with it. I'm fine with what I'm doing! I'm not your patient, leave me alone and go talk to my son!"

Wow, that moment comes back to me and I remember it well. I had to defend my addiction and I made sure he knew that. I didn't want anyone taking away my fun and especially calling me out on what I was doing to myself. At the time I thought, "How dare him?" But now years later, I feel differently because I know he threw me a lifeline that day and what did I do? I slammed the door shut, locked for good. I had a golden opportunity that day to change my life and I didn't. I would use this story to teach others about getting help, but at this time, I was focused on having a personal pity party, that no one but me wanted to attend.

CHAPTER 19

I STARTED USING THE CREAM right away on my hands and arms, and it didn't seem like a big deal for the first few days. After that, I noticed my skin starting to burn and I was getting sores, big red ones all over. It was extremely painful and impossible to cover up. I called the doctor's office and was troubled by what was happening to me. This little cream was causing a lot of damage and I wanted to make sure I wasn't having a horrible side effect. The nurse told me this is normal and to use it until my skin starts to turn a deep red and then stop because I don't want scarring to happen.

Wait a minute, are you telling me I burned my skin for years to look good, and this is what the treatment does is burn my skin? This is completely ironic. I didn't feel pretty or good about "this type of burn" but look what I did all those years, decades to come to this moment. I have since used the cream on my face, hands, arms, legs, and chest. The way the cream works is it only burns where I have pre-skin cancer. If I put it on an area that doesn't have any, it won't burn there. Unlucky for me, anywhere I use the cream, it burns my skin. Over the years, the cream has changed and I am now using a stronger, more aggressive cream that at one point cost $3,300 a month (not what I paid, but that was the cost) and I have used it since October 2011 with hardly any time off. I use it because I have actinic keratosis (pre-skin cancer) everywhere on my body. It makes sense because I never covered up, but I also never knew about the consequences. I had never heard anyone talk about sun damage or the effects of tanning until now. I was learning about a "secret world" I thought where all these bad things happen but who really knows about it, other than the people unfortunate enough to have it happen to them. I was now one of them.

Chapter 20

I HAD TO DO A treatment in December of 2011 (over my winter break), and I had talked to a friend of mine whose son had this PDT (Photo Dynamic Therapy) done on his face for acne. She told me that he said it was like a tanning bed. I made the appointment and I took my husband with me for support. I was feeling uneasy and uncomfortable with all these "new" things I had to do to my skin and he waited for me to be "prepped" for the procedure. I wasn't afraid of this treatment because of how much I "love" tanning beds, and I told the nurse when I saw her about my relief that this will be one treatment I will like. I went back with her to a room with a large, reclining tan chair. I sat down and she told me what she was going to be doing. She was going to rub "medicine" on my face (which looked like a glue stick) and then I had to go to a room in the back for an hour and ten minutes. *Not a problem so far*, I thought to myself.

When I got back to the room, there was one small dim light at the end of the room and they had magazines to look at. So far, so good, the only thing that was happening (this treatment is only done on the face) was the "medicine" was drying, and it was making it hard to move my face, but no pain at all. I was going to be okay, I thought, even though I hated using the cream, this one was going to be easy. I was relaxed and anticipating getting the warmth of a tanning bed again. I missed going there; it was like visiting an old friend who always made you feel welcome.

After my "waiting time" was over, the nurse popped her head in the room and asked me if I was ready to go. I said good-bye to my husband, and I told the nurse, "Yes, I'm ready. I've been waiting for this one." She took me down the hall across from the room we started in. We walked inside, and I saw another tan chair and a large tri-glass contraption that I guessed would be going around my face. She told me to pull back my hair and rinse off my face with water, which I did. There was a mirror by the faucet, and I remember taking a quick look at myself before I sat down in the chair. She moved the machine around my face and gave me goggles to protect my eyes, which I put on right away. I was all ready to go, bring it on! She was still in the room and she gave me two things to hold. One was a spray bottle full of water and the other was a little fan.

I told her, "I don't need these, you don't understand I like tanning," but she told me that "I was going to need them." She told me the procedure would take seventeen minutes and forty seconds. Then she left the room and turned off the regular light and turned on the blue light (blue-light therapy is another name for this) and without a moment of hesitation I began spraying my face with one hand and fanning it with the other while I screamed out for help. The pain was greater than what I had ever imagined. The only thought going through my head was "I'm going to die in here" and I couldn't take the physical pain at all.

I couldn't move because the blue light was completely swallowing up everything, and I felt the skin on my face begin to burn off. It felt like acid was being poured over my face and the water and fan did nothing to alleviate anything other than to get my top completely drenched. My screams were "help me," "won't anyone help me," and "I'm dying in here!" I don't know how long it took the nurse to come in, but I wanted out now; this is torture and I can't take it. She walked in the room, and even though I couldn't see her, I begged her for help.

She asked me, "Do you want me to stop it?"

I said, "Please, you can do that, I think I'm dying, help me!"

She said if she stopped it, it would only be temporary because it has to go the full time of seventeen minutes and forty seconds. She said, "Do you need a break?"

"Do I need a break? Are you kidding me? I'm suffering, can't you hear me?" I asked her—no, begged her to sit with me and hold my hand. I knew I did not want to be alone and I was feeling, for the first time, regret of what I had done to myself. Tears of pain and remorse were flooding my vision, and I only remember her saying, "I can't stay with you, but I'll be back when it turns off." My screams turned to cries and prayers for help and forgiveness for what I had done. After the machine turned off, she did come back in the room just as she promised. She removed the machine from around my face and told me I needed to come back to the sink and wash up. My shirt was fully immersed with the water that I had used to put out the fire "on my face," and I walked slowly over to the faucet still crying because of the trauma I had just been through. I looked in the mirror and saw not me, but someone with a completely raw, turnip-red face. The tears instantly came forth and I washed my face and put on sunscreen while she was discussing with me how to care for myself when I went home. I was told I could not leave my house for two days and that I could not sit by a window, lamp, or go near my oven. I walked out of the room and my husband met me in the hallway. I was inconsolable and weak after fighting for my life in the "torture room."

We walked out of the office and I had my coat covering my face, partly for protection and partly out of embarrassment. The first time I had this procedure done, it took two full weeks to heal. I did not leave my house, and I did not want anyone to come over. I had a lingering fear of ever having to do this treatment again. After your face is burned severely, it does heal slowly. It is different than a burn from tanning, though; this burn is much different because it comes with humiliation. My face did heal but only after new skin came to the surface and lots and lots of peeling. I was grateful that I had the time off, and when I saw the doctor again, she liked what the results were but I was told I would have to do it again two months later. She still saw many pre-cancerous spots and she didn't want them to become skin cancer. That's what my life is now—burning my skin to get rid of any pre-skin cancer spots so that the skin underneath is hopefully healthy and cancer free. The next time I did the procedure I was not alone; I would never go in that room alone again.

CHAPTER 21

To say that I was terrified of going through this PDT treatment again would be a total understatement. I knew I had to move forward and this was a consequence of my choices, but I also knew what I was in for this time. I was going with a friend to an event and I was telling her all my "skin issues." I shared my fears with her and how ashamed I was of myself. My addiction was still under the surface, but I was so busy living in pain and fear that tanning was the last thing on my mind at this time. After all, it was still winter and I had not indoor tanned for four months at this point. She saw that I was feeling sorry for myself and I was becoming depressed. I was struggling with mental, physical, and emotional pain, not just from the treatments but also with the reality of not being able to be dark or tan anymore. The color of my skin had faded, and I was having a hard time adjusting to the "new me."

We were driving and talking and I felt better finally being able to let down my protective barriers around myself. She suggested an idea to me that at the moment seemed inconceivable. She asked me if I had considered sharing my story with others so they can learn about the dangers of tanning. The first thoughts in my head were "Are you kidding? This is my dirty little secret," and "What will people think of me?" I wasn't a speaker, not that I was shy, but this was airing out your dirty laundry for other people to see and judge. I thanked her for mentioning it to me, but I quickly changed the subject and that conversation dissipated in the car. She did a huge favor for me, though, without me asking. She knew I was afraid of the procedure and so she asked if she could pick out some songs for me to listen to in the room so I could concentrate on something other than the pain. The day it was going to happen, she came into the waiting room and dropped off her CD player and a CD made especially for me. I thanked her, gave her a hug, and waited for my turn to go back. Once again, my husband came with me and I was feeling apprehensive and afraid of the pain I was going to go through. I also brought a book with me this time.

I enjoy reading Joel Osteen books and I brought the book entitled *Your Best Life Now* to read in the dimly lit "holding" area. Because I had to be in there for over an hour, I tried to keep my mind occupied with positive thoughts, but at one point, I put down my book and ran out of the room to the nearest bathroom. I closed the door behind myself and began sobbing into my hands, not wanting to do this. I took about fifteen minutes in there, and I was not sure if I could "make myself" do something that I found so repulsive. I managed up the courage that I needed to walk back to the holding area, and I sat and read the same chapter again and again. I felt better because I knew I would not be alone this time. I prayed for protection from the pain and to not be alone. I was comforted by the words I had read, and when the nurse came for me, I had my "armor" on. Once in the room, I plugged in the CD player and followed the routine from the last visit. When the nurse was getting ready to go, I asked that she push the play button on the CD player before she left. She hesitated and then asked me if I wanted her to stay with me. My prayers were answered, and I almost said "no" but I stopped myself and I told her, "Yes, please stay with me." She hit the play button, gave me my spray bottle filled with water, the fan, and the nurse sat with me the entire time and talked to me—that's all, just talked. The pain was there, but not as intense as the first time and I felt powerful and protected by my prayers. The pain did not make me cry, and I felt consoled by her, not judged. In the background, the music selections were inspiring and uplifting. I was not alone. I don't ever have to be alone again, I thought. When I walked out of the room, my husband was expecting me to be the same as before, and instead I was smiling under my bright red, raw skin and happy that my prayers had been answered. It still took a few weeks to heal, but after that discovery I knew that I did not have to face this darkness alone. I have since had to do this PDT treatment one more time, and this time, I asked my daughter to come with me and be my support, which she did.

The third time, I had both my daughter and the nurse stay with me and we all three talked while I fanned myself and sprayed water on my burning skin. I was also able to reflect on the experience to be able to explain to others what "it" feels like. I can describe it like this. When you are sitting in the holding room, the medicine that they put on your skin soaks deep into the layers. When the "blue light" hits your skin, it is burning from the layers under your skin, not on the surface. That is why the fanning and water do nothing to end the pain of burning. It feels like needles, hundreds of them hitting you from under your skin at the same time. Prayer made me believe that I am never alone, and I did not know that the idea my friend gave to me would completely change my life and take my darkness into light.

CHAPTER 22

I DECIDED TO TALK TO the eighth-grade health teacher at the middle school where I live. It was in February of 2012, and I thought that I should try and warn others about what I had learned before they had to live with the consequences as I do. She is a nice, kind-hearted person, and when I told her a small portion of my journey, she was intrigued and told me she would think about the idea and get back to me. I was excited yet apprehensive because I was not a public speaker, and I wasn't sure how I could convey my knowledge in a way that would impact young people. As I waited to hear back from her, I continued on with the monthly skin checks and more painful reality checks (treatments). Another treatment I have had to do on several occasions is to have my "spots" frozen. If the cream doesn't work on an area and I have used the cream for a few months and the "burning" from the cream doesn't create new, softer skin, then I am given the option of making an appointment for this "new" and "quick" solution. I have done this process many times in the past six years and I mainly have this done on my hands. That is my worst area and the one that I continually try to hide by wearing long sleeves all year long. It is a far cry from the way I used to be and I am reminded daily of my "new normal."

I go in for the appointment and the doctor brings in with her a vertical, silver cylinder with an attachment that looks like a small hose. I tell her what I have been doing and she proceeds to "freeze" the spot or spots in my case, which immediately "burns" my skin and forces me to cringe and say "bad words" to get through the initial force of pain being bestowed on me. She sometimes goes back two to three times on the same spot in order to insure a good result. The frozen spot turns quickly into a blister, which lasts for weeks and is painful and unsightly to look at. I have also had spots frozen on my forehead, legs, and arms. In fact, when I see her, I usually tell her to "go to town" because of the cost and the healing time involved. I give her free reign to do as many as she can see in our short time together. I am told to set up my next monthly appointment, and I go home and I am again reminded of the price I pay to have been "pretty." Even after the blisters begin to descend, I am left with large, red sores everywhere that are visible to everyone. I have been asked by students that I have worked with and also adults if I have AIDS, or if I have an addiction to heroin. I am never offended by these comments; I just tell them that I have a skin condition to which I am usually told to "go see a doctor." I have also asked students if I can use their pen or pencil and sometimes they don't want me to. They tell me that they are afraid of "catching" what I have. I never get upset; I have *no one* to blame but myself. I just hope that I can have the chance to explain my story to let others know the dangers that I never knew or wanted to know. I received the email from the teacher and she wanted me to come and speak to her students. The door was opened, and I did not know until later how healing this experience would be for me.

CHAPTER 23

MY BIGGEST PROBLEM AT THAT time was once winter was finally over and spring was pushing its way into the air I "got the feeling" again. The feeling I'm referring to is to be out in the sun and for a brief time forget that I have pre-skin cancer everywhere and just be able to relax again. Even though I stopped indoor tanning, as soon as the season switched to spring I looked for my friend, my very used plastic lawn chair. Even though it was years old, I never wanted to replace it. Why would I? It worked for me and it was molded to my body. It was hung up on a hook in my garage, and when I got it down for the first time since my "diagnosis," I forgot about all the problems my skin had been through. I didn't want to be outside for a long time, just enough to get "that feeling" again of contentment. I brought it out, wiped it off, and proceeded to relax. I put my swimsuit on, laid down, and I applied a little bit of sunscreen on my face, hands, and arms. I felt at "home" again and I was taken back to a time I had forgotten about. I was silently thrilled and eager to experience the tranquil moments again. However, the minute I laid down the sun was shining brightly on my skin, the same skin that has sores and red spots everywhere. I tried to push out the thoughts of fear and worry but I couldn't do it. I tried lying over on the other side and again I was reminded that this "was" my life but this is not my life now. I couldn't do it; I had knowledge now. With all the information I had been given, I knew that I could not expose my skin to the sun anymore. Inside I was a frightened child, wanting to cling to the life I had, but knowing the door had been closed. Thoughts going through my head were "What's wrong with me?" "Why can't I do this?" I cried because of the loss I felt inside. I cried knowing that I didn't want to continue this deadly game. At that moment, I was so confused, not sure whether to listen to the warnings I had been given or to welcome an old enemy back into my life. I chose *me*. I took the lawn chair that I had such a strong, emotional tie to and gently put it inside the large, green garbage can. I walked inside and looked in the mirror to see what damage I had done to myself, afraid of my doctor finding out what I had done, afraid of everything! It took me two more tries to finally be able to say goodbye to my "old" life, my "old" chair. I didn't try using it again, but I wanted to keep it as a memento of my previous life, just as something I can look at and remember how my life used to be. But I knew that throwing that chair away meant I was hooked on being healthy, caring about myself and finally putting an end to my addiction. The addiction that I knew was still inside of me, fighting to stay alive. It took everything I had that day not to run out to the garbage can and rescue my chair but I had to let it go. If I was to start living again, I had to break ties with my bad habits and that was the start of my new path, my new "normal."

CHAPTER 24

THE EMAIL FROM THE TEACHER told me that I would be talking to three health classes for forty-five minutes each. The students were in eighth grade and the teacher stated that they had just finished their disease unit. I knew she was taking a chance on me, and I didn't want to disappoint anyone, especially myself. I had never done anything like this before and I started printing out pictures of me after I had used the cream and what my face looked like after the second PDT treatment. I also picked up some brochures from my doctor's office and I started preparing myself for the "talk." I worked at the middle school during this time in an after-school program so I knew that some of the kids would know me, but I did not say a word to any of them. I wanted the element of surprise to be on my side. It was the spring of 2012 and I knew at that time I was still feeling afraid, the fear of the unknown, and unsure if I could bring myself to tell my story in a way that would impact anyone.

I started writing out what I was going to say onto note cards. I also wanted to use a video to show before I talked to give them a preview of what I was going to share with them. How do I begin talking about something that is so "personal" and how do I say it without breaking into tears? I read my written words again and again both silently and out loud. Even though forty-five minutes isn't a long time, how do I keep their attention for that long about something that they probably know nothing about? I knew it meant so much to me because I was the one going through everything, but I needed them to "feel" what I felt. I knew that I needed to get my point across from the start and keep them hanging on every word I spoke. To others around me, it probably seemed like a far-fetched idea, being able to "touch" or "reach" young people in a way that would change their perspective on both tanning and addictions. I felt I had nothing to lose; after all, if it didn't work out, at least I gave it a good try. The big day came; the trial phase of what I hoped would propel me into a new world, a way for me to heal myself and to help others.

CHAPTER 25

WHAT A LONG AND WINDING road my life has been. I recall telling some of my "friends" that I had skin cancer and their reaction was either one of great support or considerable sarcasm. If I felt secure in my relationship with them I could open up and probably talk "too much," but if I felt the least bit insecure I would hide my "pain" and "suffering" from them. I know that most people who have an addiction are not able to "see" the effects until it is probably too late. Because mine is on my skin, I can see the damage that I have done to myself long after my tanning addiction has stopped. I love this saying: "Your skin is like an elephant, it never forgets." This is a quote from a video about skin cancer, and it is something that is constantly playing in my mind. It is a simple reminder that it can take decades for you to "see" what you have done to yourself.

I started tanning at the age of ten, and I did not see the effects of what I had done until I was forty-seven years old. Even then I did not stop tanning until one year later, when someone was finally able to stand up to my addiction and allowed me to see the light, the truth. I now have a brand new perspective on how precious life really is. Everything that I used to take for granted is now cherished in a brand new way. Clouds and sunsets which gave me the feelings of sadness and disgust are now looked at with a new appreciation. Spending time with my family is now a top priority and cherished. I want my son and daughter to be proud of me and not worry about me anymore. Even though I can't promise them anything, they know that I am a new person and that they mean the world to me. I have asked my family to forgive me for my past decisions and I pray that they do not step into the darkness of any addiction. That is my hope for them. They have been with me every step of my journey and continue to remind me that I am a strong, deserving, and caring person. After the way I treated them and showed no regard for their feelings when they were younger, I am humbled by the way they forgave me and still allow me to share my victories and sorrows with them. Their love for me is never underestimated or taken lightly. I am here today because of love, a love that is pure.

CHAPTER 26

I AM GOING TO ADMIT something to you. Every time before I speak to a group or a class, I pray before I go. I pray for strength and for the words to make my time with them matter. I pray for them to hear me and to be inspired and "touched" by my words. The first time I spoke in front of a group of students and every time I speak, I feel nervous, but I also feel powerful. It is a great feeling to be in front of others and give them a chance to make better, safer choices than you made for yourself. I have changed my presentation over the years but the first time I went I had no idea how I could make a difference. In my mind I dealt with the phrases "Why would anyone want to listen to me?" and "Look at all the mistakes I've made."

Now I see that by showing "my life" and admitting "my mistakes," I am breaking down barriers or walls. I am no longer a slave to my addiction and therefore I am not afraid of telling the truth. Fear does not stand in my way; I show a vulnerable side to myself that in most areas of my life is hidden. I am able to be honest and sincere and I am rewarded with empathy and the hope that the students will not make the same mistakes that I have made. I also saw that it is okay for me to be "real" with them and show them pictures that scare and repulse them. The day I walked into the small, rectangular-shaped room I saw faces of confusion and interest. The teacher introduced me and had written my name on the white board in the front of the room. My time cannot wait; my time is now.

CHAPTER 27

MY FEARS OF TALKING IN front of anyone quickly disappeared that day. I had them from the moment the video started until the entire forty-five minutes were up. They saw a side of me they had never seen before, a person who had made bad choices and was standing in front of them confessing their transgressions openly and without hesitation. They were glued to me and to my experiences in a way that humbled me to my core. Some of the students would be brought to tears and the look in their eyes told me that they "got" it. The teacher was sitting at her desk and I would glance in her direction as I scanned the room, wanting everyone there to know I am talking to them and to them alone.

At that time, I passed my pictures around the room and the brochures for them to view while I talked about my ugly past and my uncertain future. At the end, the students clapped for me and the teacher came up and gave me a compassionate embrace. I would do this two more times that day and I was hooked, hooked on the high I received from letting go of my apprehensions and making myself an open book. No longer was I a victim of my circumstances. I was free at last to change my sadness into hope, for myself and for others. After I was done with all three classes I was given a potted daffodil, a large signed thank you card and a feeling of unbridled enthusiasm. If nothing else was accomplished in my life, this would be one of the greatest experiences I would ever know. I was no longer bound by my shame, I had conquered my fear, and I was unstoppable. I left that day and I had a hard time containing my excitement. My days of isolating myself in my bedroom, alone and broken were to be no more. I had a purpose in life, and it was to share my story with others and it gave me a reason to believe again. My addiction came in last to who I was becoming. No one paid any attention to "that"; they were focused on "me." The person who I thought was a loser, but not anymore. I could not lie down and take the pain silently anymore. That would give my "old self" the reason to give up. I was never going to be the same. This was a game changer and would change my direction in life.

CHAPTER 28

I USED TO LOVE GETTING my picture taken when I was younger and "tan," but now that I see the scars from the battle I am in, pictures are no longer my friend. However, I wanted my husband to take many pictures of me, for a purpose. I could use those unsightly reminders as a way to educate young people in a way that words alone cannot. I saw every procedure now as a way to teach, to show the ugly side of tanning and I could tell them about the deadly lies an addiction entices you to believe. I shared this "new" and "thrilling" adventure with my doctor, and she was pleased that I found a release that was both healing for me and helpful for others. It was the only bright side of the hardships I would have to endure.

As I look back at older photographs of me in my younger days, I see a person who was carefree, self-absorbed and clueless. Those photos used to be all that mattered to me, and now they are regarded as a story, my story. I received positive feedback from the teacher and her students and I quickly saw that speaking is rewarding. At the end of the school year I felt sad that I had to wait to speak again until the following November, it was going to be so hard. The time went by and I remember struggling with the alluring sunshine over the summer. I had started to wear sunscreen but not always and I didn't think it would make a difference if I did or didn't. There were still bumps along my path, and I was still seeing my doctor once a month but now I clung to the future in a whole different way. I was being relied on to tell my story and it thrust me into a positive force, and it started to impact my personal life. I had found a purpose to care, to live my life to the fullest, and to appreciate my struggles.

CHAPTER 29

I WENT BACK TO THE middle school in the autumn and in the spring. I was starting to find a rhythm with my words and the students were listening, fully receiving the information I was giving them. The pictures were still being passed around, and I had their complete and undivided attention. In fact, now I was given the opportunity to talk to two classes at one time in a big, open area of the school and I craved every moment of this setting. The fear of failure was not with me; I was armed and ready to fulfill what I had come to do. Every eye in the room was watching me, closely studying my every move. I found it was okay to show emotion and by talking about my choices I would become choked up, but I was safe there. Judgment was not invited to join me, and just like before, I saw students become emotional and sometimes have to leave the area. In fact on one occasion after I spoke I was sent down to talk to a student privately. She knew me and had become so upset that she went to the guidance office to be consoled. I walked down the hallway and through the double doors. Inside one of the rooms the girl was inside, clearly uneasy about what she had just heard. I walked in and she ran up to me and hugged me while she cried. We sat down, and I did my best to tell her that I am okay, I'm a fighter and I'm going to be just fine. I could tell that she was responding to my direction, and I allowed her to express what she was feeling. Before I left that day she and I made a pact. I promised her that I would never ever tan again and she promised me that she would always try to make good, healthy, and safe choices for herself. We pinky swore and once again hugged. She cared about me and she knew that I cared about her also. She now knew my secret and I was so glad that I was allowing myself to shed my "old self."

CHAPTER 30

IN THE SUMMER OF 2013, I made a decision. I was going to make phone calls to other schools to see if I could bring my story and firsthand experience to their health classrooms. I made all my initial contacts over the phone and I received both positive and uninterested feedback. Because it was the summer, the teachers were not in the buildings and I was told that they would contact me in the fall if this was something they were looking to pursue. I have a full-time job so I knew I couldn't do this as much as I would like to, but I wanted to take my story to other young people. I needed to get out of my comfort zone and expand my viewing audience. I was also inquiring of high schools because I thought they would need to hear the "truth" about tanning especially at their age. In the fall, I slowly received phone calls and emails wanting to know more information about my presentation. It was exciting to make new contacts and to "push" myself into a new avenue. I had the teacher at the middle school get a hold of the health teachers at our local high school. I wanted a chance to speak to a new group of students, to see if I could talk and get through to young people who were older and more at risk for the consequences of tanning and addictions. I would get my opportunity, but not until the second semester of the school year. I wasn't feeling discouraged because I was still speaking, reaching out, and perfecting my words and becoming more confident in what I was doing.

CHAPTER 31

I MADE MY MONTHLY TRIP to the doctor and I found out that I would have to get another PDT treatment on my face in February of 2014. I made the date for the day before Valentine's Day, what better way to celebrate than by turning my face into a bright red color. I was still using the cream on a daily basis and at times I would have to go in and have "freezing" done on my hands and arms. This would be my third time doing the treatment on my face and even though I wanted to disagree with her I knew she wanted the best for me. This time I took my daughter with me and I remember feeling so embarrassed while she and the nurse were in the room talking to me as my face was being burned by this incredibly powerful, blue light. The only thing different this time was I wanted to be able to document in my mind the whole procedure.

Now that I am talking to others, I wanted to be accurate with my information. Instead of just "dealing with the pain," this time, I focused on how I could explain it to them and make it "real" and give them a blow-by-blow account. Even though my daughter and the nurse were talking to me and to each other, my whole mind-set was being able to explain this experience with great detail. I included this "recent procedure" to my notes and I talked to the classes just before and after I had it done. Because it was so fresh in my mind, it gave me the ability to make my case even more powerful on what not to do. When it was done, my daughter drove me home and again I sat on my couch, hiding from any light. It still took time to heal and I was so jealous of anyone that didn't have to live my life. Even though I made the choices I just wanted to be left alone, and to stop being in pain. I was so sick of seeing my doctor, and many times I have expressed this to her. She has said the same thing back to me. We both want this to end, but I know that would take precious time and much patience. I need to vent sometimes and many times I have cried.

Most of the time I cry by myself because I don't want to burden my family any more than I already have. One of the new things that happened when I did my presentations to the eighth graders was the teacher started having the students write me a takeaway message. At first I didn't think much of it, but when I opened the first batch of letters, they brought instant tears. The only way I knew they "got it" before was by the attentiveness they showed me, but now I have letters written to me confirming what I needed to know. Their words were powerful and simple. They shared with me secrets about themselves that probably no one else knows. This small gesture changed the way I shared my story. These letters were personal and some were long and others were short, but it didn't matter; they were mine. I could pull them out and read them when I needed a hand to help me up. I shared them with my husband and I recall many times sitting on our couch, each of us fighting back tears as we read them. I could hardly wait to receive these letters that the students wrote to me. Each time I went back to speak I felt more and more at ease. I was making a difference and I knew I needed to stretch my wings to reach others.

I was doing better until March of 2014. I had a spot on my left hand that I had used the cream on, and it wasn't being affected by the aggressive treatment like the other spots had. In fact I called up my doctor and I told her that something was different with this one. I made an appointment to have the area "frozen." I don't know why they call it freezing when in actuality it burns, so bad in fact that it makes every filthy word reach my mouth and explode like a cannon. She froze other spots on both of my hands, but nothing compared to the excruciating pain on that one spot that was the size of a pencil top eraser. Each time she came back to expose it to the "freezing gun," I had a hard time physically enduring the pain that was being subjected upon me. She froze it three times before I was able to pull myself together and leave her office.

As soon as I left, the blisters became obvious and swelled up all over the tops of my hands. Even though I have had this done several times I have never become used to it. Each time feels like a "new" experience, and I am brought back to feelings of shame and wanting to wallow in my pain. Nothing can speed up the healing after your skin is treated in such a harsh way, but I tried to stay positive in my thoughts. I would try to have my self-talk be "this will be the last time" and "you are stronger than this." I had gone from seeing my doctor every month to once every three months and now it was once every six months. I remember her telling me a few years ago that if I made it to once a year, I would be in a very good place. I was halfway there, and I kept convincing myself that I could do this.

Thank you so much for sharing your story! Just know you have reached me and I will take your words to heart. My mom had several spots removed but unfortunetly died this past may at the age of 53 from a cardiac arrest. So your words mean more to me than you will know. It feels like your words are exactly what I needed to hear! Thank you so much again! Stay strong!

I also have suffered from addiction, and as a reccuvering addict I want to tell you, Great Job!! Addiction is a very hard thing to conquer, but we are proof that it can be done! Stay strong and be grateful that your past experience has brought you to appreciate things in life that most people over look. Keep fighting.

I Just want to tell you that I loved your presentation. You are such a beautiful and inspiring person. I loved how you were so brave and honest with your life story. I pray that in future you get to share your story all across the world to let others be aware of the seriousness in skin cancer.

God Bless you!!!

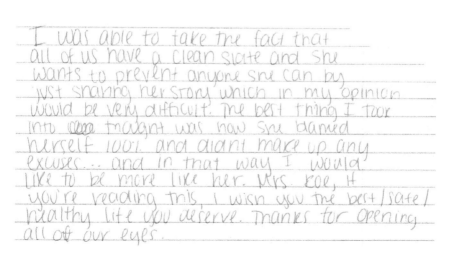

I was able to take the fact that all of us have a clean slate and she wants to prevent anyone she can by just sharing her story which in my opinion would be very difficult. The best thing I took into consideration thought was how she blamed herself 100% and didn't make up any excuses... and in that way I would like to be more like her. Mrs. Roe, if you're reading this, I wish you the best/safe/healthy life you deserve. Thanks for opening all of our eyes.

Mrs Roe,

Thank you so much for telling us your story. It was very moving. It struck a chord with me because my mom usually pressures me to tan because I'm so pale. Your story made me realize how damaging it is to my skin, and I finally was brave enough to stand up to her and tell her that I didn't want to tan. I told her about how insecure it was making me, and I told her about your presentation. She agreed not to bother me about it anymore. Your story was very informational and it showed me that I need to protect my skin, no matter what others say to me.

Mrs. Roe
- Your presentation had me in tears. You are such a great speaker, the way you told your story, the tone of your voice, just everything tied into your message and made your story stick with me. You inspired me to do better and help others realize that you have one chance in life and you can't mess it up. You are a beautiful lady, and I know you're here for a reason. Your suffering will help others not make bad choices. Thank you so much. You are seriously so strong, I would of gave up.. God bless you.

I really enjoyed having Mrs. Roe in class. She really opened my eyes on how dangerous tanning can be. I used to tan in tanning beds before they made the law that you had to be 18 or older, and I always told myself I would go when I turn 18 but now I realized you dont have a second chance with your skin like you do with most things. If Mrs. Roe ever came back I would tell her thank you for opening my eyes and she kind of turned off that voice in my head telling me to go back to tanning beds when I'm 18. I don't think I could ever thank her enough for that.

Mrs. Roe,

Knowing you before your presentation and not knowing you had such a condition changed my whole view on just about everything. You're such a strong lady! Being able to share your story is just awesome. Some people are afraid to come forward about their problems, I'm glad you did. I hope treatment gets better so you don't have to go through so much pain. Keep spreading your story it's touching & helping all ages. Thank you.

Dear Mrs. Roe,

I am very thankful to have had you come to talk to my class about your personal exeriences. I have a frend who goes all the way to Wisconson just to use tanning beds and sometimes I think of what could happen to her years down the line. Now, thanks to you, I can tell her how bad all of her tanning really is. Thank you for telling me of your real experiences and feelings.

P.S. I pray your pain shrinks and your voice is heard.

I think it's wonderful you do these presentations because I use to work at a place with tanning beds and did not realize it was an addiction until I worked there. I am still haunted by the fact that two men go to that place and tan EVERY DAY, for the longest time they are able. And those men are a bright red all the time. I wish you could present to them.

The speech that Mrs. Roe gave us, really made me think about how much sunscreen I put on in the summer. One thing I will take away from the speech is putting on more sunscreen. I never really thought about it before, but from now on I will put sunscreen on when I go to the pool, playing outside, or whenever I'm out in the sun for long periods of time. Another thing I will always remember from the speech is, respect yourself and your body. Many girls do things like tanning to feel pretty. Now I know that you don't have to because everyone is pretty in their own way. I want to thank Mrs. Roe for teaching me about the dangers of tanning and what skin cancer can do to your body and to your life. I will certainly pass it on to others.

Before I knew that it was bad to tan, but I did it any way. After you told us your story I will never tan again. You have really opened my eyes to how bad it is to tan. I'm going to not only stop taning my self, bw I am all so going to tell others of your story and try to stop them from taning. I will pray for you and thanks so much for coming and telling your story. Many people really don't understand just how bad it can be but your story let me know just how bad it was. Thanks again, I hope the best for you.

Mrs. Roe...
   I appreciate you coming in and talking to us! You are very inspirationae and gave some good advice. I'm very sorry you have been through all of that. You have come so far, so Please don't give up! Each day you will become stronger and you'll keep inspiring kids all over this county.
      Thanks for being so brave!

Dear Jana,

Thank you so much for coming to our class and sharing your story. it definately made me look at the sun in a new way, and I thank you for opening my eyes to the harmful effects of sun exposure. I already went out and bought new bottles of sunscreen and I put one in my backpack for when I eat lunch outside, and also put one in my car. I really appreciate that you took the time to speak to us. I thought about how many times I have been badly sunburned in my life and I can really only think of one time, but now I know that any burn can be harmful. I know that you have another surgery coming up and I am hoping that everything works in your favor! You were such a positive influence to have in class and I hope you come back to speak to more students at BHS.

Dear Jana,

Thank you so much for coming and speaking to me and my class. Your story was powerful and impactful. You opened my eyes and made me consider things I had never thought to consider before. I find that very impressive. You are one of the strongest people I have met as well as influential. They way you took your pain and hardship and directed it towards others is adimirable and inspiring.

Again, thank you. I hope and wish for you not just a happy today, but a happy everyday.

Dear Jana,

First I just want to say you are the bravest women I know. Thank you for coming to my school informing my class and I about how serious skin cancer was and sharing your story with us. I know it must've been hard for you to talk about your experience with skin cancer; I could feel your emotion through your voice, and I could hear the hurt and pain in your voice while you were speaking and it really moved me. Before you and Brett told us how serious skin cancer was I had no idea, but I'm glad I know now because I can tell others and people I love and care about. The major thing that stood out to me in your presentation was when you said your skin will never be healthy again. Before you even started to tell us you had skin cancer I thought you were so pretty I don't see a women who has skin cancer I see a strong, brave women keep fighting and stay strong.

Dear Mrs. Roe,

Thank you so so much for sharing your personal life story with us, I know everyone in the room, including myself, were so engrossed in what you had to say and even got emotional for you. Your message really struck me with being thankful for what I have + who I am no matter if I have tan skin or fair skin because I need to appreciate the health of it. You have some crazy guts to tell all of us what you've been going through, you are truly making an impact! Praying for your strength.

I use to tan when I was 15 and I loved it, I was always told I wasn't pretty enough, not skinny enough, never enough. I pushed my boundaries when it came to weight and appearence you opened my eyes to so much more than I ever thought. I was actually planning on tanning after school today for my boyfriend and my couples pictures next week and I now know I don't have to, and I won't I have so many friends and family members I've lost to cancer I participate in the Relay for life every year and I've always felt like such a hipocryte. you've given me hope to know I'm stronger than I think I am. I loved your story. you really changed my life

Thank you

♡ Hope you stay strong

Dear Mrs. Roe,

Thanks a lot for the speach, I never knew tanning could be so hurtful for the body. In fact when I was little, down in Arkansas (age 12) I thought I wasn't tan enough so I would lay on the back of the boat w/ no sunscreen on, but now I know the consiquences of tanning, I'm not going to tan like that, or tan at all for the most part, I dont really care how dark or light my skin is. Again, thanks for sharing your story, I know it may have been hard for you, and I hope to see you doing this around the country.

Dear Mrs. Roe,
Thank you so much for coming in yesterday to talk to us about your skin cancer and tanning addiction. It made a huge impact on me. After listening to your presentation, I am definitely going to make a change in my life. Starting this summer, I am going to make sure to always wear sunscreen. Last summer, I went days when I didn't wear sunscreen because I thought I didn't need it anymore. From now on, I will always cover myself in sunscreen. I also will make sure to not stay out in the sun to long. It really hit me when you said that tan skin is damaged skin. It made me wonder why in our society we believe that tan skin is beautiful. Thank you so much for sharing your experience. You probably saved my life by sharing what you have to go through. I too have also thought that I would never get skin cancer. My friends and I would joke that one day I would because I would get tanner than them. At the time it had seemed funny, but now after your presentation, it isn't' funny. I can likely have skin cancer if I don't change what I am doing. I know how hard it is to have to do all you do everyday to keep from having skin cancer but I ask that you keep fighting. With your presentation and speaking to different classes, I know there will be at least one kid in every class you talk to who will have such an eye opening experience as me. You are saving lives by having this presentation and are helping younger generations to protect themselves. I told my mom about your presentation and she wanted me to thank you for saving her daughter's life. She also had noticed that every summer I was getting a little more obsessed with how tan I was. I would fight her and tell her I didn't need sunscreen or as much as she wanted me to put on. Because of your presentation, now she won't have to fight me about having sunscreen on and preventing skin cancer. Thank you one more time for saving me. It means so much that you go out of your way to go to different places and have this presentation. You are an amazing person that people should look up to and learn from.

BURNED: MY JOURNEY THROUGH ADDICTION

Dear Mrs. Roe,

Thank you for coming into speak to us. Thank you for showing how strong you have been, and sharing your experience with us. Thank you for trying to warn us of the dangers of the sun and tanning beds.

As you said we all make mistakes, and we either live and learn from them or continue to make them. Thankfully you were able to stop, and I find that incredibly courageous of you. I myself have an addiction that also ruins my skin, but in a completely different way. After your presentation I felt very heartbroken that I ruined my skin as you said you did yours. Many scars will never heal, but it all depends on the way you look at them.

I find it empowering that you continue to fight your battle everyday even after quitting your addiction. I can understand how tiring all of that is. I knew what you meant when you talked about throwing away your lawn chair; I have been through a very similar process that I have yet to fully break.

Thank you for showing me that it is important to take care of your skin, and overall yourself. I hope you continue to fight your battle, and I am hoping the best for you. I hope one day all your treatments will be over or that they will significantly lessen. I hope that one day that I can break my bad habit as you broke you addiction. You are a source of inspiration, and a light in an ever so dark tunnel.

I learned that even after so many years of being stuck in something that I can break it, and that it is never too late to get help.

I will always make sure to take care of my skin from here on out. Not only to try and help it recover from the damage I have done, but from the sun as well. I used to not wear sunscreen for my own personal preference of hating the feeling. I now know that just because I don't like the feeling or smell I would hate to have damaged skin.

All skin is beautiful naturally tan, pale, dark, all colors and undertones as well. Everyone no matter the skin tone should take care of their skin and I hope that society will one day break the stigma that having tan skin is broken.

Once again thank you for coming in, and for being an inspiration in more ways than I think you even expected. You are strong and I hope you continue to be strong. Thank you for showing me that I can be too and that every person and every skin is worth taking care of.

CHAPTER 32

EVEN THOUGH SHE HAD FROZEN the same spot three times, I noticed and felt something strange. This was not healing, and in fact it had gotten larger and more defined. I could sense it was growing underneath my skin, and I was scared. I knew I needed to call once again, but this time, I knew what the next step was. I knew I would have to get a biopsy done and I made the appointment knowing that I had no control over anything. When I see her my time is quickly used up and she gets down to business. My hand was prepped and numbed and the biopsy was taken and sent away to be examined. I was told they would call me within a week or two and let me know the results. I prayed and hoped for the best, but in my gut, I knew this would not be good. The phone call came as I was leaving my job, and even though I wanted the words to be different, I was told, "The results came back and it is squamous cell carcinoma." They also told me that she wanted to do the surgery within the next two weeks, this couldn't wait.

After the initial shock, I called back the next day and scheduled the day and time. I would have the surgery in April of 2014 and I looked up information about this type of skin cancer that I had not had before. I found out that it is more aggressive than basal cell carcinoma and once again I found myself struggling with the news. The morning of the surgery, my husband wanted to come with me. I told him, "I'm a big girl, I can do this myself. I'll be okay." As I drove there, I looked down at my hand, angry that I had to deal with another surgery. I was brave and the one thing that kept me strong was being able to share this new situation with the students that I talk to. I wanted them to grasp and see the "reality" of my situation and I took pictures as my hand was prepped for the procedure. My skin is thin due to the years, or decades, of burning my skin to be tan and when I looked down, I was amazed to see a balloon like swelling of the area and a large purple eye drawn on it. Inside the purple eye drawing, there was a small, red circle. I was told that she would have to dig deep and wide for the cancer that was already spreading under the top layer of skin. That is why my hand was expanded. I looked down and saw the "spot," the evil spot that had caused me so much pain. I was given multiple injections to numb my hand, and I asked the nurse to get my phone for me. She thought I had to make a phone call and I told her I wanted to take a picture before the doctor started cutting. You are probably not aware that every treatment, every biopsy, and every surgery I am wide awake. The only thing they do is numb the area, but you are not asleep.

In the room they put on relaxing music, and I was asked if I was comfortable. I was in no pain and I trusted my doctor completely so I said, "I'm fine, I'm ready." I had my left hand to the side and even though I could have watched, I chose to look the other direction the entire time. We conversed and I tried to get the "sounds" of the surgery out of my head. At one point I experienced pain and I was not shy in not telling her that I could feel what she was doing. She immediately grabbed a syringe and it was numb once more. She told me when she was done and then she stitched up the cut. I was completely numb and the nurse applied a large bandage to the area. It was over and I was told to keep the bandage on for two days and then I could remove it. I left and I drove myself to my job, still numb from all the shots I had been given. In my mind I thought "this wasn't bad, what was I worried about?" I couldn't feel a thing, but that was about to change.

CHAPTER 33

I WAS AMAZED AT HOW good I felt and even though my hand had a large, oversized bandage on it I couldn't feel anything she had done. I knew she had dug for the cancer, she had shared that information with me, but for the moment, I was feeling relieved that I was pain free. When I left work I started to feel a dull, achy pain, and by nighttime, the pain was intense. Sleeping comfortably was out of the question. How do you sleep when you can't put your hand down to your side? The pressure was so strong that anytime I put my hand down, the pain became unbearable and I would quickly raise it up to my chest. Tears from frustration and my discomfort couldn't be stopped. I wanted to go to sleep because only then would I get relief. That night was difficult and long. The next morning, I went to work but I couldn't believe the amount of pain I felt compared to the day before. To ease my pain, I had to hold my hand up by my chest all day and I was physically drained just from doing that. At my second job, I shielded my hand from the middle school students, protecting it from any further harm. I still didn't "see" what the surgery looked like on my hand until the next day.

I drove with my husband to pick up a prescription that I was to take to prevent any infection. As he was driving, I slowly started peeling away the bandage. I stopped myself and waited until we got home to finish the task. It was time to take it off and I fought hard to contain my emotions as I stood there not believing what I was seeing. I saw a large stitched up line extending two inches from the top to the bottom. My hand and arm were immersed in black and blue color and swollen from the surgery. I took the pills that I had just picked up and threw them across the room. I fell to my knees and sobbed screaming, "I can't do this anymore, I can't live like this! What did she do to me, why did she have to cut so much?" is what kept running through my mind.

My husband tried to once again console me and I would have no part of that. I felt violated and abused and I didn't want him to make me rationalize my thoughts. He gave me the time and I was able to release all the pain and scariness of my "new reality." I had to come to grips with the way my life is now as I stood there in disbelief. The same pills that I had thrown against the wall were now being picked up by me as I sat on the floor trying to find them all. I then remembered that everything can be used as a teaching tool. I stopped crying and told my husband to grab his camera as I began focusing on using this to help others. He took several pictures of my hand by itself and then beside my other hand to show the size difference. He also took a side view because my hand was now shaped differently. I even grabbed a ruler and held it up to my stiches. Seeing this two-inch scar red, swollen, and raw would do better than anything I could talk about. Pictures say so much and I was going to say plenty. The pain and sadness were still there but being able to focus on anyone other than myself became my refuge. I thought the worst was over but I was incorrect. Every day became a new nightmare as I saw the stitches starting to pull away from my skin and expose the large, disgusting gaping hole in my hand. Every other day I went to my doctor's office and saw the nurse. Because they are not able to stich the wound again, they would apply a small piece of ivory tape to try to keep the wound from gaping outward. It did not work and they were talking to me about reconstructive surgery if this didn't start healing properly. The top of the wound starting closing, but the bottom part was open and not coming together like it should. Trips to the doctor became a part of my routine for weeks afterward until it finally started closing. This ordeal was draining in every way possible. I thought I was out of the woods until less than six months later.

CHAPTER 34

IN APRIL OF 2014, I was contacted by the high school health teacher. He had talked to the health teacher at the middle school in our town and wanted to give me a chance to speak to his classes. We set a date and this opportunity was different because I would be talking to a total of six classes throughout one day. I knew one of the teachers but the other teacher I would meet the day of my talk. I was excited and it was a new challenge for me, one I was ready to explore. I had just gone through so much with my hand and I knew that this "fresh audience" would be a good way to see if I could do this in front of new eyes. That morning, I went to my knees and I prayed for God to give me the words to say and to make my speech powerful. I thanked him for this great opportunity and to keep pushing me forward. I wanted to make a difference, and as I walked into the door of the school, I knew I was not alone; I had everything I needed with me.

I packed my notecards, my pamphlets and pictures that could be passed around the room while I spoke. As I walked through the hallways, I was stopped by former students who wanted to know how I was, and to offer me hugs of support. I embraced this time because it lifted me to where I needed to be as I stood in front of several rectangular tables. Behind every desk were faces of people, kids wearing headphones and playing on their cellular phones. As they piled in the room, I looked each of them in the eyes and greeted them anxious for the bell to ring and my time to begin. The teachers were both in the room and I felt comfortable but well aware that I had to be on. This again was a moment that I needed to be strong and meaningful with every word that I spoke. Time was not on my side, even though forty-five minutes seems like a long time, to me it is never enough. I was introduced and the students were told to put everything away, even their precious phones because I was going to talk to them about something that could change their life. They reluctantly followed the directions given and even though there was no spotlight I knew it was my time to shine—let's begin.

Chapter 35

I AM IN COMPLETE AMAZEMENT that each and every time I get the chance to speak I have my audience captivated in a way that touches me so profoundly. This day was no different. Once the video is finished playing, I begin taking them on a journey with me as I tell them about the different types of skin cancer, how much importance I placed on tanning and the way I treated others, especially those who cared about me. I am brought back to that day ten years ago when my son's dermatologist threw me a life line. How I wish I would have said those two simple words that day that could have changed my life, "Help me." Those words are so simple, yet so incredibly hard to say. He never again talked to me about my skin; we only discussed how to help my son. I tell everyone I speak to about his kindness and how horribly I treated him, simply because I was an addict and I didn't want anyone taking away my fun. I am embarrassed and ashamed of the manner I spoke to him. I am sure he felt humiliated and I knew I owed him an apology. I wrote a letter to him in December of 2014 telling him what I am going through and that I never forgot that he tried to help me.

I also let him know that I am teaching others about the dangers of tanning and I share my story to prevent them from going through the pain and regrets that I live with. I sent it a few weeks before Christmas and my gift that year was from him. He wrote me back and he said he was proud of me and that he shared my letter with his staff. His words brought tears to my eyes because he is committed to never giving up on anyone, maybe like me they will find the light. Those types of gifts are the best ones, they are priceless. I cherish his letter, and I bring it with me every time I speak as a reminder of how important it is to share my message. I won't give up on myself or on anyone I have the privilege to speak with. Together we are working on the same cause, in different ways but we both are on a mission to save lives.

CHAPTER 36

THE FIRST TIME I SPOKE at the high school, it became clear to me that this is where I belong. I saw faces of disbelief and horror as I stood there being real with them, more real than any text from a book could be. Every class, no matter how large or how small, was completely entranced. The teachers were taken back that it was so quiet you could have heard a pin drop. I captured my audience completely and fully. My words were precise and exposed the reality of my life. No, you cannot look at me and see what I have been through. In fact, at one of the schools, I heard two students speaking to each other before I started talking. They didn't think I could hear them as they were guessing what my addiction was. They convinced themselves that my addiction was to smoking because I have a deep voice. I stood there, very aware that you can't always see what someone is struggling with. It gives me more conviction to treat others with kindness because you never know what someone is going through. Not everything is visible to your eyes; sometimes you can only see it with your heart. As I glanced around the room that day, I saw a young lady who looked to be "popular." As I started talking, I watched her body change and at the end she was toward the wall and in the shape of a ball. As the students were leaving the classroom, she came up to me and asked if she could hug me. I said "yes," and as she hugged me, she told me she would pray for me and when she was older she wanted to be just like me. I asked her for her name and I felt my legs weaken by this kind gesture. I have been talked to by many students over the years. I don't take that for granted in any way. Yes, I give to others but I also get back so much. In fact at one school I had a girl tell me if anyone ever makes fun of me, she will beat them up. She is in seventh grade and she meant every word. I told her I'm okay and that no one makes fun of me. It made me see the power of the words I speak. They get it; they all get it.

CHAPTER 37

I spoke that day with such conviction that the teachers asked me to come back at the beginning of the next school year. They reassured me that what I am doing is so helpful, and once again, when I received the letters, it humbled me to my core. The honesty and compassion of their written words still resonate in my mind today. I was able to take my story to a middle school and another high school in two different cities close to my town and the same thing happened. When I began talking, the class was silent and taken back by my boldness and direct approach on these two difficult subjects, addiction and skin cancer. That summer I started to seriously apply sunscreen to my heavily damaged skin, not thinking that it would help, but I should at least give it a try. By the time I saw my doctor in October of 2014, I looked my doctor straight in the eyes and without any hesitation I said, "I'm cancer-free, you are not going to find anything on me." I said it with such confidence that by the time she started easing into my personal space, I did not shy away from her like I usually did.

For once, I felt assured that the surgeries were over and that I had come out from the dark hole I had been in just six short months ago. She noticed the skin on my hands and arms and asked me what I had been doing, that they look better than they ever had before. I shared with her that I am "really" applying sunscreen and she said, "Keep it up, it is helping." Okay, make sure you read over this again and again especially if you are one of the many people out there who thinks sunscreen doesn't work, it does! If sunscreen can help my skin and mine is so damaged, think about what it can do for your skin.

If nothing else, please start using sunscreen. Don't be stubborn about it; isn't your life worth that small gesture of protection? Let me be clear also that up until this day, I had never heard that my skin is better, and I honestly never thought I would hear that. She looked over my body and did not see anything, but then she started to examine my face and I could feel her finger gliding over a spot on my forehead as she looked at me and said, "I'm sorry, you have a spot here." I begged her to leave me alone, to pretend she didn't see anything, and I gave her permission to find one anywhere else but not on my face. Unfortunately, that could not happen and she shared with me the news that once again I would have to be prepped for a biopsy. They worked quickly as they numbed my forehead and took a small portion of skin, which they enclosed into a small plastic test tube. It was a normal procedure for me, but not on my face, I thought. Over the years, I have had spots frozen on my face and I have even used the cream on many occasions, but I wasn't ready for this; let's face it, I'm never ready for this. How can you prepare yourself for the word "cancer"? It just isn't possible. As I left her office, I did feel a sense of peace because God is leading my life and once again I prayed. I prayed for God to give me the strength to be able to handle "His will" and that if it is cancer, I would use it as a teachable moment for others to learn what not to do. I am reminded again of how lucky I am and that if I let God be in control I have nothing to fear.

CHAPTER 38

THE DAYS OF UNCERTAINTY WERE replaced with the reality of my condition when I received the phone call from the doctor's office letting me know that the results came back and it was once again basal cell carcinoma. The only good thing about basal cell is that it is the most common type of skin cancer and it grows the slowest. That is the good news; the bad news is always "surgery." Once I hear those dreaded words, I know what I have to go through and I try to focus on having positive self-talk. I say to myself, "I will be okay and I can use this experience to help others not make the same mistakes I have made." I kept having those thoughts repeat themselves over and over again while I sat there trying very hard not to feel sorry for myself. This was probably the only time I did not cry when I got off the phone with the nurse. I opened the door of my supervisor's office, which is where I went to get the privacy I needed and I told my friend Becky, "It's cancer, but I'm okay. I'm going to take pictures and be able to help others learn from my mistakes." I meant every word I said as I stepped back into my classroom and began interacting with the students in the room. I am once again knocked down, but there I will not stay.

CHAPTER 39

As I SAT IN THE room with my doctor going over the procedure that would replicate the surgery on my hand, I felt my mind drifting to a different place, away from the scariness of having a large scar on my forehead, away to a peaceful place where I am healed. I didn't get the chance to stay in that place long as she tried to comfort me as she showed me the exact location of the area she would be cutting. I had heard from a friend of mine about a surgery called Mohs. It is supposed to be a less aggressive surgical alternative to the standard procedure that I had on my hand. I openly discussed this option with my doctor, being careful to explain to her that because it is on my face I wanted to have the smallest scar I could possibly get. She understood and gave me the name of a doctor in a town about forty minutes away from me. He was able to do this type of surgery and I would need to see her afterwards for a recheck.

I scheduled the appointment and even though I never met the doctor before the scheduled day I looked at my husband and calmly but assertively told him, "I'm ready, let's get this over with." I always tell both of our children about any "procedure" I am going to have. My son lives in Washington, and because he is so far away from me, I try to be extra strong for him and reassuring. The place I went to is large and in a busy city. By the time we parked and took the elevator up to the second floor, I was working overtime on making the only thoughts in my head to stay positive. I checked in and was taken to an area behind the "normal waiting room." It is where you go when you need to have surgeries, and as I scanned the waiting room, I saw many faces, not much different than mine waiting patiently for their turn.

I was looking at a magazine and listening to the morning news when my name was called. My husband accompanied me through the doors and into a room where I would be asked questions from the nurse. I answered them all and was told about the surgery. Because it is Mohs, they only take out a small portion at a time. If the doctor gets it all the first time, I can be stitched up and on my way. However, if after the first try there is any cancer under the microscope, they would keep taking more and more until they do not see any cancer. This could potentially be an all-day event. I asked a few questions, but honestly, the anxiety of being wide awake and having someone cut into my face stopped me from asking everything I normally would. My husband stayed with me as long as he could and when the doctor came in, I felt relieved that this would be over soon and hopefully it will only take one try. He was kind and put me at ease as the procedure began. My face was covered except for the area he would be cutting. I did not feel anything other than the pokes to numb my forehead. I explained to the doctor that I would be taking pictures of the entire surgery from start to finish because I share my story of skin cancer to young people. He was intrigued with what I was telling him and he asked if I would be willing to give him copies of the pictures for the website he has. He told me to check out the website and give him my thoughts as he finished with the first phase of the surgery. My husband was brought back to the room and snapped a photo of the circular hole in my forehead. After the picture was taken, a large piece of gauze was put over the incision and I was told it would be at least forty-five minutes to an hour before I would know if I was done for the day. During that time in the holding area, I checked out his website at www.checkyourskin.net and I maneuvered in and out of each of the areas while I tried to distract my thoughts. They have a video on their website, and as I watched it, I couldn't fight back the tears that were streaming from my eyes. It was a powerful video of people sharing their experience with melanoma, and it shook me and reminded me that this is real. It was about five minutes long, and I don't remember how many times I watched it, but the result was the same each time. I broke down and cried. I told my husband that this will be the new video that I start my talk with—this will add power to my purpose. We also called our son and he didn't know we had it on speaker mode. I heard him say to my husband, "This is it right, dad. Mom's going to be okay?" My heart was officially broken that day hearing my son's voice with so much concern and not wanting me to go through any more pain. I cannot promise anyone anything past today, but I try to leave tomorrow in God's hands.

CHAPTER 40

IT WAS EXACTLY AN HOUR when they once again took me through the doors and they had good news for me. The doctor had removed all the cancer and now I could be stitched up and go home. Whew— what a relief, especially after seeing so many people in the holding area go back more than once. I saw people who had their nose, ears, and cheeks cut and I was so happy that mine was at least on my forehead. The doctor came in, and I told him that his website was amazing. I also let him know that the video on his website moved me to tears. We talked as he stood over me while I once again was numb. At one moment, I could feel the stitches going in, but it was quickly diminished as he sat me up, and I had my husband take a final picture before I was given strict instructions to keep this "unicorn like" covering on for two days and it couldn't get wet. No shower for me, I thought, but this time, I chose not to look at the picture that was taken. I was feeling queasy and nauseous partly due to feeling so anxious about the outcome. I thanked him and told him, "I hope I never get to see you again," as I held my husband's hand while we walked down the hallway and past the holding area still filled with unlucky patients, still waiting to hear their "good news."

CHAPTER 41

RELIEF CAME OVER ME AS soon as I sat in my car and buckled my seat belt. I knew that I didn't see what my forehead looked like before they put on the oversized white gauze, but I was hopeful that it wouldn't be as bad as I thought. The pain was not present until a few hours later and then it was excruciating. I could not be consoled as I wept once again and waited for the night to become day. I would not be going to work for the next few days, but having time alone at home meant my mind would wander and that is not always the best thing for me. I had the procedure done on October 30, and before the pain set in, I told my husband I could answer the door on Halloween, but by the next night, I was in no mood to be seen by anyone. I just wanted to wake up from the nightmare I was having and be myself, just some sense of normalcy and no pain. By the end of the two days, I was apprehensive and frightened at what I would find under the wad of white. I told my husband to have his camera ready as I unveiled my forehead. My forehead was swollen, and because of the large covering, I didn't notice that. My nose and eyes were swollen besides being black and blue. I looked like I had been in a fight and lost. I noticed the red scar on my forehead and I held back my tears as the pictures were taken. That was the only solace I had, use this to teach others, thank goodness I had that. It took me for a short time away from the present, away from the reality that I had to live with. Smile for the camera.

CHAPTER 42

THE HEALING TOOK A WHILE for my face. I had to keep it covered up and I did share with some students that I had a procedure done, but unless they hear my presentation, they have no idea the trials I have overcome. One of the worst days I remember is when I went for my two-week checkup at the doctor's office. I took off the bandage and the nurse made comments such as "It looks great" and "Wow, that healed up nicely." I, however, did not make the same comments. I didn't see it the way she did, but I wish I could. She then put a large mirror in front of my face and told me how to use the cream to lessen the appearance of the scar. I *hate* looking at myself in a mirror, let alone one that is directly two inches from my face. I pretended to agree with her just so this misery would end. When she was done, I couldn't wait to be gone, and even though they were extremely kind, I never wanted to step foot in that building again. As I'm sitting here I'm trying to cross my fingers and toes.

CHAPTER 43

THINKING BACK TO THAT TIME, I was getting the "itch" again to take my story to a different location. I had spoken with a friend of mine and she made a suggestion to me. She had a cousin that worked at a school about an hour away from where I live. She gave me his contact information and we were finally able to meet in person toward the end of the school year. He worked at an after-school program and I let him know that I was interested in bringing my message to his students. He told me they were "tough," "hard," and that they didn't listen to guest speakers. He said he had tried it before and his students treated them with such disrespect that they would leave in the middle of their speech. I sensed from him that he did not feel completely confident in my ability to "control the room," but I told him I could do this and that if anyone would be wasting their time it would be me, not him. We set a date, and I was excited but a little nervous because of the information he had given me. The day I was to drive there, he called me a few hours before I was to leave and told me I couldn't come, his principal didn't want me to go there, he felt it would be a waste of my time. He also said, "It wasn't a good idea. They would never listen to me." I was upset, but I kept my composure and I reassured him that "speaking" is what I'm passionate about, especially when it comes to the two topics I would be talking about—addiction and skin cancer. He reluctantly put me on hold and said they wouldn't be responsible for how I was treated. I agreed and as I hung up the phone I knew that I had to be "on" the entire time today, no holding back!

CHAPTER 44

THE DRIVE THERE WAS NOT as pleasant as it should have been, and the entire time I practiced my speech out loud. I didn't care what anyone thought; I wanted to be ready for whatever came my way. I saw the entrance to the high school and there were very few cars there. My friend who suggested I come here accompanied me for both moral support and to hear my plea. We parked and she called him to meet us at the front doors. We shook hands and he led us back to his classroom. For the moment, the students were in another room making a snack so I had a few minutes to get everything set up. This was my first chance to speak to a very diverse group of students, but skin cancer can happen to any skin color. Of course if you are white/caucasian like I am your chances are much higher, but no matter what your ethnicity is, you are still at risk. As they walked in, they barely paid any attention to me while they kept talking loudly to their friends. It was a good mix of boys and girls, and I could tell that the teacher would not be able to do much to support me. Even after the teacher told them to have a seat and to stop talking, they kept sitting on their desks, playing on their phones and talking loudly. My confidence started to waiver a small amount until after he introduced me, then it was "my turn." Some of them were sitting in their seats facing forward toward me, but many of them were still paying no attention to the new person in their room, me.

I have a loud voice and I said, "Hey, I'm here to talk to you about something that could save your life. I'm not getting paid to be here.

I'm here because I care about you, even if I don't know you. This is the way we are going to play. It is now my turn to talk and your turn to be quiet. If you have a question, raise your hand and I will call on you. If you don't, then I don't want to hear your voice." They started to sit down and they were holding each other accountable. I didn't have to say anything more. We watched the video and then I began my story. There were a few questions and I was happy to answer them, but for the most part, I had their attention and I commanded the room. I could tell by the teacher's body language that "this" doesn't happen, but today it did. I talked for one full hour and they didn't disrespect me once. At the end, I was putting away some of my props, which included a bag of grapes and a bag of raisins.

One of the students asked if they could have them and I said "Sure" and I threw both bags to her. I saw my friend to the side, trying to hold back tears because she never knew the obstacles I had to go through to get here today. I didn't ask for any letters and I went up to the teacher to thank him for letting me come here today. As we were talking, sharing what just happened in that room a girl, probably around sixteen years old walked up to me. Without saying a word, she handed me a folded up piece of lined paper with a smiley face on it. I told her "Thank you" and I asked her if I could open it up and read it. She barely looked at me but she said, "No, not until you leave." I thanked her again and I put it in my bag. The teacher walked out with me and I told his class, "Thank you for listening to me and have a great summer." Some of them responded back to me and some of them could have cared less. While we were walking down the hall, the teacher shared with me that he had "never" had his class listen to "anyone" before, especially for an hour but he said, "You did it." I asked him about the girl that gave me the letter and he said she was sweet, but very shy. He also said that she doesn't open up to people, that she just keeps to herself. As we came to the doors to walk out, I couldn't help but to open up the letter and read it.

This is what she wrote to me: "thank you for coming and talk about what you've been through. I wouldn't be able to do that. I honestly think you are beautiful even though you went through so much I'm not just saying that. I have an issue with my looks to and try to be good looking …and people keep on saying I'm not ugly I always say no you're a liar. Made me think about it when you talked about this."

If you don't pay attention to the grammar usage and really read what she's sharing, it's beautiful. I cherish this letter from a girl who didn't even sign her name. What's important is that she "got" what I was talking about and was willing to open up to me and share this we me, a complete stranger. Even if it was written, she communicated with me and trusted me enough to give me this gift. How special did I feel after I read this? Words cannot even begin to convey my feelings, my thoughts, and my knowledge that I have to keep reaching and putting myself and my story out there for others to hear. It is important, I have hand-written proof.

CHAPTER 45

LET'S FACE IT—I LOVE TO talk, really share and expose myself as a past addict to break through the barriers that keep people away and disconnected from us. I'm learning that by being open, honest, and real, I can reach kids, especially those who really need someone to look out for them. Don't we all need to feel connected to someone? I was absent from my own life for so long and I have a lot of catching up to do. My world was so small and dysfunctional, but that was the only place that I found safety and acceptance. My addiction has taken away so much from me, but slowly I am finding myself again. It seems like I can see for the first time, my eyes are wide open and even though my life is scary and overwhelming at times, I can feel now and I allow myself to face my challenges and not run away from them. That's what my addiction did; it took me away, away from my life. I was so far down that I couldn't even humor the thought of getting up, and breaking free. I want to share one of my favorite Bible verses: "I can do *all* things through Christ who strengthens me" (Philippians 4:13). What a loving and strong message for all of us. Don't go through your life alone, share it with others and bring joy and hope just as we are given.

CHAPTER 46

THIS PAST YEAR HAD BEEN fairly quiet and calm. The last surgery I had was in October of 2014. Even though I had no "new" calamities to share by putting my pictures in a power point it gave me the freedom of movement and of finding ways to get my message across even stronger. I always bring props with me when I speak. I bring grapes and raisins to use the analogy that grapes are hydrated and not damaged until they are in the sun and then they turn into raisins. I use the words "dehydrated, damaged, and wrinkled" to get my point across and it works. The letters confirm that it is easily understood by all grade levels.

My favorite prop is a watermelon baller. Yes, you heard me right, a watermelon baller. My inspiration comes from the doctors I go to see. I was given that idea from the doctor who did the surgery on my forehead. I saw the "hole" and I asked him how he got it to be a perfect, round circle and he said, "You know a watermelon baller. Well, I use something similar to that." He gave me the idea and I went to a local store and picked one up. Nothing gets a class to "gasp" better than that. I see heads turn away when that photo comes up, but then when I add the prop it gives a lasting effect, hopefully one that cannot be forgotten. That's why I do this, I don't do it to hear myself speak or to just be another adult lecturing; I am educating them. I want them to be aware, not frightened. One of the greatest lines in the video to me is one that I repeat during my time with them. Someone says, "Your skin is like an elephant, it never forgets." That is a simple line but powerful. It can take decades for you to see the damage you have done, but that doesn't mean your skin is not paying the price. With other cancers, you cannot see what you have done, but I am reminded every time I look at my skin, the consequences I was willing to choose to be tan. Oh, if only someone could have talked to me when I was younger, maybe I would have made better choices than I did. But that is living in the past and in regret and I can't do that—I've come too far to make that mistake.

When I first met my doctor in October of 2011, I had to see her every month. I finally jumped the three-month hurdle, and then I was at six months and I could hardly contain my excitement. She had told me some time ago that my goal was to make it to twelve months. At the time that seemed so far out of my reach, but in the summer of 2015 that is exactly what I heard. In fact, I made her repeat it out loud to me as I tried very hard to keep my emotions in check, but that never happens. My tears this time were tears of joy as she told me to call if I needed to be seen sooner, but if not next summer would be soon enough. I called my family right away and shared this wonderful, unbelievable news with them. We had all been through so much together and it felt so gratifying to be able to give them "good" news today. It was a few months later in November that a spot showed up on my hand that caused me to start using the cream, specifically on that one area. Even though I could see that the cream wasn't working I refused to call her office to set up an appointment. I knew what would happen, she would take away my twelve months, something I had worked so hard to get. I dismissed the spot and kept using the cream knowing that I was fooling myself but I couldn't go back, not yet I thought. Give it one more month, then two…

CHAPTER 47

IT WAS ONE MONTH LATER that I forced myself to call up her office to make the dreaded appointment. Even though I tried to deny it, I knew this wasn't good; this was not going to be what I wanted to hear. I tried to replace positive thoughts with the scary, negative ones, but in the end, I knew it and she confirmed my fear. The biopsy that she did came back once more to be squamous cell carcinoma. The ironic part of this is that the spot was right next to the other surgery I had on that same hand almost two years ago. The scar was almost completely invisible, and here I have to do this again. I did not take it well and I cried, screamed, and cursed not feeling that this is fair. "Why me?" I said again and again, not wanting anyone to take away the anger I was feeling.

I was supposed to be done, I thought. I hadn't had a surgery for eighteen months and I was okay with that. I had paid my dues, leave me alone! I didn't want to use any more of my life lessons; I wanted this to stop, to be over. Unfortunately I am spiraled into a grief each and every time I am thrust into the ugly side of skin cancer. I am tired and I want to be left alone, but that is not my life now. I was hurried to get this over, but at the same time, I knew that it would be horrible and painful. The appointment for my surgery was on March 1st and 2nd. She was able to do the same Mohs surgery on my hand that was done on my forehead. I knew the scar would be small, but that was little consolation for me.

The first day I went back with the nurse and was made quite comfortable. The doctor came in and the pre-surgery routine had begun. Since I will use this as a teaching lesson I had to take pictures. Number one it takes me away from where I am, and number two they work better than words at times. I was numb, and when I finally looked down, it reminded me of the surgery on my forehead. All I saw was a circular hole in my hand with blood spilling out from it. I snapped my photos and was told to go to the front waiting room. They had to once again make sure they removed all the cancer before I could leave for the day. I spoke with other patients about our experiences, and before I knew it, I was given the okay to leave. I would have to come back the next day for stiches, but right now, driving away from here was satisfying. I kept waiting that day for "pain" to find me but it never did. I felt great and other than the large dressing on my hand, I couldn't tell that anything had been done. The next day was the complete opposite. As soon as she was done stitching up the wound, I again took some pictures. I left and it didn't take long for the aching, dull pain to set in. I was in no mood to do anything; nothing could prepare me for the reality of my life and the pain that comes from my consequences. But in the long run, this keeps resonating in my mind "I can see clearly now that my addiction is gone." I am forced to feel, think for myself, and live in darkness or light, and I will always choose light.

CHAPTER 48

IT HAS BEEN SEVEN YEARS since I began my fight. My life is different now and different doesn't have to be a bad thing. As I am typing this, I am trying not to look at my arm, hand and legs that have large, red sores on them from a freezing treatment that happened just a week ago. I usually wear long sleeves, but right now, my arms are exposed and I struggle with living in my skin on a daily basis. One of the letters that a college student wrote to me said, "Knowing that someone else struggles with being in their skin helps me feel less alone." We are connected and yet that person is probably twenty years old and I am fifty-five, but we feel the same way about our skin. How unfortunate that many times people judge us from what they see on the outside instead of looking at the beauty that lies within each of us.

I also have a few items that make me feel safe on a daily basis. One is a man's light blue long-sleeved shirt. I actually have two of them and they are always in the back seat of my car. After I found out about my condition, I would have panic attacks while driving because I knew I could not afford to have my skin exposed to the sun whether in my car or outside. I went to a store with my husband and I was looking for a shirt for him, but when I tried it on it was mine. It is big on me, but that's what I like most about it. I wear it in the car when I am driving if I don't have long sleeves on. It covers up my arms and my hands, but I am still able to drive. Even if I'm not driving, I pull it up front with me to cover up. I also wear it when I ride my bike or mow the lawn. It is a life saver for sure and I call it "my go-to shirt." I have an old blue hat and for me it has so much significance. I never protected my face and I would have never worn a hat, but I received it for free a few years ago. I wear it all the time when I'm outside mowing, riding my bike, or walking. I thought I had lost it, and I was broken, inconsolable, and crying. I now know why, it's because that worn-out used hat makes me feel safe in a world where I don't have that feeling of safety. Thank goodness the hat was found and I bought a back-up one just in case anything really happens to my trusty hat. In fact I feel like I play better tennis when I am wearing it. Maybe it has more power than I give it credit for. Yeah, right!

Also sunscreen is something I don't leave home without. I never, ever wore sunscreen but now I won't walk out of my house without it's' protection. I buy kids sunscreen because it has the two ingredients we all need—zinc oxide and titanium dioxide. It is only found in kids sunscreen, why is that? I have absolutely no idea. It doesn't make any sense, but that's the way it is. I use an SPF 50 and when I ask students how much it costs the answer is $6 or $7. That's right $6 for protection and to date I am well over $35,000 for treatments, surgeries, etc. This is definitely a no-brainer. Wear it and don't fuss about it. I have the best sunscreen for my face. It is a powder that I picked up at my doctor's office. It looks like I'm putting on makeup but I'm protecting my face. It was a little expensive, around $100, but I put it on all the time and it has proven to work. I carry it with me all the time and like my sunscreen I won't leave home without it.

One more thing I want to discuss is self-tanners. I don't use them anymore, but there is nothing wrong with having the feeling of being tan, without the risk. Because I have sores on my skin, almost always, it is hard for me to find a time to mess with putting it on all over. I have also chosen ones that made my skin an orange color, so for now I'm okay without using them. When I think back to when I was twenty years old, I was always seeking approval from everyone on the way I looked and I hope you don't find yourself on the same path I chose. Yes, I chose my life and I try very hard to stay focused on my future and allow my past to stay where it belongs, behind me. At one of my appointments I decided to ask my doctor a few questions, but I was afraid of finding out the answers. On this day, I felt brave enough to know the truth. The first question was "Am I the worst patient that you have (as far as how damaged my skin is)?" and I was told "No, I have patients that have had forty-plus surgeries" compared to my ten, and some of those patients she needs to see every two months because their condition is so severe.

Okay, that answer made me feel better, onto the second question. I had to ask about the cream that I put on my skin to burn the pre-cancerous spots I have. I wanted to know if there are any long-lasting effects. She asked me if I had ever read the pamphlet that comes in the box and I said "No." She said she was glad I didn't. She then told me the cream works like chemotherapy, but instead of ingesting a pill, I use a topical. She explained that it is chemotherapy for my skin and the medicine in the cream attacks the abnormal cells, which make my skin red, swollen, and burned. As I sat there feeling a little scared she patted my leg and told me that I am doing the best thing for my skin by using this. She continued by telling me, "If you didn't start using the cream years ago, I would be very afraid for you." Even though I felt I was prepared for her answers I started feeling like I had gone too far but then I asked, "Have you ever had any patients die from skin cancer?"

Her answer was "Yes, I have had several."

I then wanted to know, "What types of skin cancer did they die from?"

Her response was "Melanoma and squamous cell carcinoma." She knows that I have had squamous cell carcinoma twice on my left hand and in almost the same exact location so she made sure to tell me that they had "large" areas, not small like mine. My last and final question is the one that would affect me the most. Here it is, "How old was the youngest patient you had that died?"

She quietly answered me by saying, "Twenty-six."

I said, "What did she die from?"

And my doctor said, "*He* died from melanoma that was located on his face."

I said, "That's so young" and "That's terrible" and she replied, "Yes, it is the hardest part of my job." She then gave me advice which I'm sharing with you right now, "Tell everyone, this is real and people die from skin cancer." Enough said.

CHAPTER 49

OVER THE YEARS, I HAVE also been asked some hard questions. The first one I remember is what if I tan one time, will I get skin cancer? The only thing I could say to that is a quote from the video that I show before I speak. This is the line that I answer that question with "Your skin is like an elephant, it never forgets." I can tell you one thing for certain: anytime you get sunburned, you have damaged your skin and the effects might take decades to appear on your skin. Look at me, I started tanning at age ten and I'm now fifty-six years old and I was diagnosed at age forty-eight. My skin was showing signs of damage before that, but I just didn't notice or care.

The second question that comes to my mind is "How do you get someone with an addiction to stop?" This is something I have to deal with, and now that I don't have an addiction, I understand how my children felt. They would beg and cry to me that they didn't want me to die and my response each and every time was "As long as I die tan." I didn't understand their pain when I had my addiction, but now I do. There is nothing you can do to stop someone from their addiction—each person has to stop for themselves. That is such a hard reality, but it is so true or I would have stopped decades before I did. My advice would be to support them, be their friend, let them know you care and pray for them. This comes at zero cost to you, but your words can be powerful and life-changing for them. Never underestimate your role in someone's life.

CHAPTER 50

OVER THE YEARS, I HAVE struggled with depression, self-pity, and a tremendous amount of guilt for what I have not only put myself through, but mainly my family. Just over a year and a half ago, I saw my doctor for a regular visit. She looked at my skin and told me, "I don't think you're going to die from skin cancer." I looked at her with a blank expression on my face trying to comprehend what she meant by her statement. After several minutes, I was finally able to ask her, "What do you mean by that?" as I sat there feeling put down and confused.

She explained herself and this is what she said, "You don't understand. When I first met you, I had no hope for you. I didn't think there was anything I could do for you and I almost told you I could not help you, but the treatments have worked, and I don't think you're going to die from this." Tears welled up in my eyes, understanding what she was "saying" to me. I knew right then that she considered me to be a lucky person, someone who by all accounts had done so much damage and destruction to herself that my fate was sealed. That person was not me; I had been given a second chance, not without battle scars, but I am a survivor! The path of addiction was not to be my destiny in life. No, my fate was hampered and slowed down by my "illness," but today, I am a new person, a person no longer bound by the lies of an invisible, yet powerful enemy— addiction. I want to dedicate this book to my family for the support and forgiveness they have given me, even though it is always harder to forgive yourself. I also want to thank Dr. Fred Kemp, Dr. Amanda Friedrichs and Dr. Ashish Bhatia for caring about me and making me "whole" again, or as whole as I'll get in this life.

In my presentation, I end with two important reminders. One is to always say "*no*" to "*anyone*" who asks you to do anything that is not safe, healthy, or good for you. I am thankful to this day that my daughter said "no" to me every time I begged and bullied her into tanning. Thank you, Stacy, for being so strong and for not letting my addiction become yours. The second reminder is if you ever find yourself with an addiction, please say the two words I was never brave enough to say "HELP ME." My life could be different today if I would have done that, and for me I almost waited until it was too late.

I did not write this book for sympathy; please don't feel sorry for me. I am a lucky person. I am addiction free today because of a doctor who took a chance on me, and I will forever be grateful to her. I defeated my addiction and many people don't. I also know how strong I really am. I had the ability all along to stop the madness, but I didn't realize it until after the "voice" in my head was muted. My addiction will not silence me; I am no longer a prisoner to the lies that I believed years ago. I've been knocked down, pushed around and I have felt like giving up many times but my addiction didn't win—I did! I want you to learn from my mistakes and to be inspired to make healthy, safe choices for yourself starting today. I could stay "stuck" and feel sorry for myself but instead I'm telling my story so you can make better choices for yourself than I did. If you're reading this, you're worth it and I finally know I am too. I've had multiple pity parties and I have said many times, "I quit, I can't do this anymore," but I keep pushing forward, stronger because of the healing that comes from the ability to share my journey with others and from the light that shines within me. My skin is permanently damaged, and I try not to live in fear every day, but I have found my purpose in life and you need to find yours also. I cannot fix me, but my story can help someone and maybe that someone is you. Don't be alone in the darkness.

"Ask and it shall be given to you; seek and ye shall find; knock, and it shall be opened up to you" (Matthew 7:7). I talk and openly discuss my circumstances in order to help young people see the reality of what an addiction can do to you. Don't waste one day listening to deceit and empty promises. I'm passing my light unto you because I want you to stay away from the darkness and find hope from the "light" the "truth." I'm not giving up—nothing is going to make me stop fighting. Giving up means my addiction wins, and I am the victor in this story. Even though this is the end of my book, it is a new beginning, a new start for me living addiction free.

ABOUT THE AUTHOR

JANA ROE IS A FIRST-TIME author, and she has worked in education for over twenty years. She shares her personal story to educate and inspire young people on the dangers of tanning and how she defeated her addiction. Writing this book helped her to heal and she wants anyone who reads this book to know that they have the ability to change their lives, just like she did.

She and her husband live in the Midwest and they have two grown children.

CPSIA information can be obtained
at www.ICGtesting.com
Printed in the USA
LVHW050354060819
626587LV00020B/73/P